ONLY BELIEVE AND NEVER GIVE UP

An Autobiography

John L. Winright

ISBN 979-8-89428-450-7 (paperback)
ISBN 979-8-89428-451-4 (digital)

Copyright © 2024 by John L. Winright

All rights reserved. No part of this publication may be reproduced, distributed, or transmitted in any form or by any means, including photocopying, recording, or other electronic or mechanical methods without the prior written permission of the publisher. For permission requests, solicit the publisher via the address below.

Christian Faith Publishing
832 Park Avenue
Meadville, PA 16335
www.christianfaithpublishing.com

Printed in the United States of America

To all my family and loved ones, seek the Lord, and He shall be found.

PREFACE

WE ALL HAVE one life to live, and each person has a story to tell! Here is mine, and I pray that everyone who reads this book will be blessed. Just know, Jesus is the answer.

> Whatever was to my profit I now consider loss for the sake of Christ. What is more, I consider everything a loss compared to the surpassing greatness of knowing Christ Jesus my Lord, for whose sake I have lost all things. I consider them rubbish, that I may gain Christ and be found in Him. (Philippians 3:7–9)

Sometimes God lets us experience great pain to learn the lessons of greatest importance. Knowing Christ intimately is the most important lesson we will learn. Only believe, and never give up!
Do not love the world.

> Do not love the world or the things in the world. If anyone loves the world, the love of the Father is not in him. For all that is in the world—the lust of the flesh, the lust of the eyes, and the pride of life—is not of the Father but is of the world. And the world is passing away, and the lust of it; but he who does the will of God abides forever. (1 John 2:15–17)

CHAPTER 1

The Early Years

And when the Philistine looked about and saw David, he disdained him; for he was only a youth, ruddy and good-looking.

—Samuel 17:42

John's father, Clinton Carlyle Winright

I WAS BORN on April 5, 1944, in Defiance, Ohio, a small community in Northwest Ohio. It was known at one time as Fort Defiance. For those of you who might know your history, this was toward the end of World War II, of which my dad served in the US Navy! My parents were Clinton Carlyle Winright and Dorthy Irene (Strobel) Winright. We lived in a small two-bedroom house on 1143 Emory Street with an alley running beside it and a small yard.

New York Jets guard Dave Herman from Edon, OH

I have some memories from living there until I was between two and three years old but not a lot, some being that when it rained, my brother Bill, sister Bonnie, and I would go out to the curb in front of the house and wade in what seemed to be gushing water up to my waist, which most likely was probably only a couple of inches deep. I remember several neighborhood kids coming over to play on a regular basis. One specific story that I remember, is my mom telling us that a neighbor boy was standing at a window during a thunderstorm, watching the lightning, and was blinded by it. I never knew for sure if that was true or if she was just trying to frighten us from doing so during a storm.

The house in Edon, OH where John grew up

We often would go out to the Defiance dam and park on the Maumee River for family picnics and fun.

Back then, we had no television, so our entertainment came from an old cabinet-type radio. I remember two things being broadcast over that radio: one being the Grand Ole Opry on Saturday nights and the other being Paul Harvey daily.

It was always a real challenge to turn the knob on the radio back and forth, listening to a bunch of static, until we could get the reception needed. When we got the reception, we would all get excited and clap our hands in joy!

We spent a lot of time playing outside and entertaining ourselves with hide-and-seek, kick the can, tag, and all kinds of other things that kids did back then. Also, a highlight was the ice-cream truck that would stop by on a regular basis. We didn't have the distraction of cell phones and Internet, so we relied on these activities daily.

Around 1946 or 1947, my father returned home from the navy, and we relocated to a small farm that my grandparents owned, a mile north and a mile east of a smaller town by the name of Edon, Ohio, on what was called the Cable Line Road. This farm was 24 acres, and my grandparents sold it to my dad and mom and moved to a 120-acre farm just across the Ohio–Indiana state line.

JOHN L. WINRIGHT

My grandparents were farmers on both sides of the family. Harry and Clara Winright raised crops and milked about twelve cows by hand. Clara did all the milking. William and Eva Stroble, my mother's parents, lived east of Montpelier, Ohio, and did basically the same, but William did the milking. He was also on the Montpelier Board of Education and Jefferson Township Trustee for many years.

My ancestors on the Winright side of the family came from the Topeka, Ligonier, and LaGrange, Indiana area. I don't remember a whole lot about my great-grandparents, except occasionally going to their farm in the spring to pick berries along their fencerows. My great-great-grandfather Babel is buried at an old country cemetery not far from there. My great-uncle Roland was a very sophisticated man, who was always dressed up in a suit and tie, smoking expensive cigars. He was married to Aunt Jenny, whom at one time was his schoolteacher. He owned a farm along with his brother, my great-uncle Loyd, and they both invested heavily in stocks. Roland was also a WWI veteran.

John's great great grandparents, Bable Winright and Elizabeth (Butler) Winright

Loyd, to my knowledge, never married and lived in a small house in Ligonier, while Roland and Jenny lived in an immaculate older home in town, with all the fine wood floors and trim that homes had back then. I remember the French doors that entered their library office area. Roland and Loyd had no children.

One story I remember is when Loyd passed away, and my family was going through his belongings. They found thousands of dollars hidden in various places throughout his house.

Their sister was Aunt Nora, who was married to Uncle Dee, and they had a son named Walter, who was married to Betty. They lived just outside of Ligonier on a farm, with a river running through it. I loved going there as a child.

On the Stroble side, all I know is they came over from Germany and located in Chicago, then all of them moved toward Ohio and settled in the Montpelier area, except for one of my grandfather's brothers, who stayed in Chicago, and I believe that Christian author Lee Stroble is his grandson and is a relative since he is from Chicago.

My great-grandparents and their family on both sides started many of the distant businesses in and around Montpelier, some of which are still standing today, although most of them have been renamed.

My grandmother Eva's brother, Bunny Campbell, opened a restaurant many years ago that was called Bunny's in my hometown of Edon, Ohio. The story is told that people from all over the tristate area would go there to eat. Sometimes it was so busy that folks were lined up outside, waiting to get in. Steaks were his specialty!

John's family L-R William, Bonnie, Baby Thomas, Judy,
John Lee with their parents Irene and Clinton

Our new property at Edon consisted of a three-bedroom, two-story home that had no indoor plumbing, which was quite a change from our previous home in Defiance. It also had a barn, which we all were very excited about. Upon arrival, one thing I remember as a three- or four-year-old were the tall weeds that had overtaken the whole yard surrounding the house and the smell of freshly mowed hay in a nearby field.

After living in town on a small lot, the surrounding twenty-four acres seemed huge to me. We had to use an old outhouse to go to the bathroom and an old well pump to get water and to bring inside. We had a routine of filling a laundry tub with water on Saturday nights in front of the woodburning stove so we could take turns bathing. During the winter, we slept upstairs using blankets and coats to stay warm. There were times that we would wake up, and there would be snow on the inside windowsill.

It took us a few years, but my dad built an addition onto the house with a basement and an enlarged kitchen with an adjoining bathroom, which did give us the plumbing we needed for water to use updated and modern indoor facilities. Living in the small community of Edon was much different for us as a family. It didn't take long to find out that everyone knew everyone. It was like one big family. Back then, we had party line crank and talked to the operator-type phones. Every time you called someone or received a call from someone, it seemed like everyone on your line joined in on the conversation.

Winright Siblings 2015 L-R Bonnie (Winright) Warner, Judy (Winright) DeMuth, John and Thomas

When we moved there, it was just my parents and my brother Bill, sister Bonnie, and I. But by 1950, we were joined by a sister Judy and a brother Tom. We still only had that old radio to listen to for keeping us in touch with the outside world, but it was sometime between 1952 and 1954 when we got our first TV that we could get three local stations out of the Fort Wayne, Indiana area.

It had a twelve-inch screen, and we all gathered around it in such great excitement. Wow, Lawrence Welk on a Saturday night, cartoons on a Saturday morning, and local and national news every evening.

My older brother and sister started attending school, and I was home, eagerly anticipating when I would be able to get on that bus someday too. The bus driver was Russel Kuckuck, who also owned and operated the local Shell station on the edge of town, where we would buy our gas, etc. Several times in the spring, when our old dirt road would be too wet and muddy for the bus to come and pick us up, Mr. Kuckuck would come and get us with his personal Jeep.

Finally, the time came when I reached the age of five that I could experience going to our kindergarten for half-day sessions throughout the year. Mrs. Krill was our teacher, and it was then that I met many kids that would become lifetime friends.

One memory from those days was that at Christmastime, we kids would come down to open our presents on Christmas morning, and they would consist of one shirt and one pair of pants from Sears or Montgomery Ward and maybe one toy or something else that we had requested. We were elated with these things, along with the nuts and fruit that were on the coffee table.

I know this is much different than the world we live in today, but as I think about it, I really think it was much better for us, and we really appreciated things much more back then.

The first eight grades included kindergarten and were housed in a big two-story brick building, separate from the newer high school. Kindergarten consisted of some learning, a lot of playing, and a fifteen-minute nap time but most of all, becoming acquainted with our classmates.

As I progressed through grade school and junior high, I was blessed to have great teachers that really cared for their students and treated them like family.

It was then that my dad took a stand and said we needed to start attending a church. We did, and our family became members of the St. Peter's Lutheran Church in town. One of the first things I remember, as we sang hymns before one of the services, was my dad singing very loudly in a base voice "The Old Rugged Cross." His voice just seemed louder than anyone else's, and I loved it. We became very active, and we kids were in Christmas and Easter plays and the choir and took the required catechism classes.

Some of the most prominent families in the community attended there. And of course, all the kids that attended went to school together. As a young boy, I remember getting to pull the rope on the bell in the bell tower at the start of services to ring the bell and periodically lighting the candles on the altar! I remember, as I pulled down on the rope to ring the bell and as it returned upward, it would lift my feet off the ground. On lighting the candles at one service, our organ player, Ruth Burkhardt Parsons, told me, "Johnny, you looked like a little angel lighting the candles this morning." Several years later, while visiting her in a nursing home, she repeated that memory with me.

From there, I proceeded through the first eight years of my schooling. I participated in baseball and basketball in the seventh and eighth grades. I loved basketball, and we even put a rim up in the old haymow of our barn. I would go up there every chance that I had to practice my game.

I believe, my love of sports was passed down from my dad as he played baseball, at which he excelled, and he absolutely went nuts waterskiing at his sister's, my aunt Retha's cottage at Hamilton Lake, Indiana, just straight west of town across the state line.

During this time of my life, from the age of twelve or up, I started working on our farm and my grandfather's, along with being hired by a couple of local neighbors to help them on their farms too. We also had a neighbor, Ed Shieber, who raised tomatoes, and he had a canning factory that many local ladies worked at in a seasonal position. My brother Bill, sister Bonnie, and I would ride on the planter in the spring, placing tomato plants in a revolving wheel, which would place them into the ground as we were pulled across the fields by a tractor that Mr. Shieber would drive.

I also became a very close friend to Jimmy Fisher, who was two years older than me, and we spent a lot of time hanging out together, riding bikes to town and to school, and being in Boy Scouts.

We camped out a lot, went fishing, trapped the local Bear Creek for muskrats, minks, and almost anything else we could get. His parents also owned a business that sold silkworms as bait for fishing, and they would hire my sister Bonnie to come and count them and place them into containers for marketing. The work ethic back then was very strong, and I learned a lot about life, work, family.

My father worked at a factory by the name of the Weatherhead in Antwerp, Ohio, about thirty-five miles from home on second shift and farmed both our farm and my grandfather's farm. One of the things I did to help was to drive tractors and equipment from our farm in Ohio to my grandfather's farm in Indiana and back. It was about twelve- to thirteen-mile ride each way.

John's mother, Dorothy Irene (Strobel) Winright

My mother's biggest worry when I did this was that I had to cross Route 20, which was always busy with cars and semis. But I never had any problems with this. Back then, our tractors only traveled at about twelve miles an hour, so that trip always took an hour or so. One memory is a farm that I passed on the way to and back on these trips had a falling running spring of fresh water out by the road. Almost every time I drove by, I would stop and drink some of the finest water that I have ever tasted.

The house between his dads and grandfathers farms where John worked as a boy and would stop to get a drink for a spring fed well

Dad was a very hardworking dedicated husband and father. One thing I recall is in 1955; he came home with the first new car that he had ever purchased. It was a Chevrolet Bel Air that he got at the dealership in Edon, which was owned and operated by Mr. Reas. I believe the price tag on that car was around $1,800.

CHAPTER 2

My High School Years

My son, hear the instruction of your father, and do not forsake the law of your mother; For they will be a graceful ornament on your head, And chains about your neck.

—Proverbs 1:8–9

ENTERING HIGH SCHOOL was a very exciting time for me. I had maintained excellent grades through grade school and was ready to move on.

Our freshman year, students from grade schools in Blakeslee, Cooney, Ohio, and Metz, Indiana, came to Edon for their high school, thus increasing our class size to about fifty-seven and bringing new acquaintances into our lives. It was exciting to have to pick what classes we wanted to take.

My neighbor friend, Jimmy Fisher, bought a 1956 Studebaker Hawk and would pick me up every morning on his way to school—no more Bus rides, and we got there much faster.

I personally chose the college education route as I always wanted to be a history teacher and basketball coach. We also had started football practice in late August, which was something I had been excited about: to be on the high school team. One strong memory from that football season was a senior by the name of Dave Herman, who was one of the captains on the team. Upon graduation, Dave went on to play for Michigan State, where he won a Rose Bowl Championship under coach Duffy Dority and then was drafted by the New York Jets, where he then went on to win a Super Bowl, alongside Joe Namath, with Weeb Ewbank as coach.

I was so impressed that someone from a small school in Northwest Ohio could go on to do such great things.

High school was also my opportunity to play basketball at freshman level. I loved this sport and put everything I had into it.

My first year in high school was exciting and enjoyable in many aspects. During the summer between my freshman and sophomore year, I worked for neighboring farmers, along with helping my dad farm both of our family farms. I loved working and just being with my dad every opportunity that I had. He started calling me his shadow because I just wouldn't let him out of my sight. He was my idol!

During my freshman year, the annual parents' night came up for our football team. It was one of those cool, crisp Northwest Ohio nights. My dad worked second shift, and I had asked him if he would be able to make it. He said he was sorry, but he just couldn't take off work. I was so heartbroken.

Finally, as we were lining up on that cool, crisp Friday night for the introduction of players and their parents in alphabetical order, I was standing at the back as my name started with a W. And as I took each step forward, the lump in my throat kept getting bigger.

I just couldn't fathom being introduced alone. Then just as my name was announced, out of nowhere, my dad and mom came up and stood by my side. He sacrificed his time just for me! What a powerful message of love that showed to a young man to hang on to and remember the rest of his life.

About a week later, after we got home from school, I changed clothes and went out to do my evening chores, which basically meant mixing up what we called slop for the hogs and pouring it into their troughs and then feeding the chickens.

It was a beautiful fall Friday (October 10, 1958) for Northwest Ohio, full of sunshine and a cloudless sky. As I was crossing from the hog pens to the chicken pens, I looked up and saw a state patrol car pulling into our driveway. I thought, *Wow, I wonder what this is all about.* I proceeded forward as both of my parents were at work, so I thought I better go see what they want.

The girls were in the house with my younger brother, and my older brother was at work. As I approached his car, he was getting out and asked me if my mother was home, and I told him, "No, she is still at work but should be here soon."

Then he asked me where we went to church, and I told him. The next thing I knew, he was backing out of the drive. And being an innocent young boy, I went on with my chores and didn't really think much more about it. In the meantime, my mom got home from work, and almost immediately, there was a knock on our door. As she answered the door, we all were standing there in our living room, and at the door was our Pastor P. Fred Huston and the patrolmen.

Our pastor didn't hesitate a moment and told my mom, "Your husband has been killed in an auto accident."

Dad was driving to work on State Route 2 about a mile north of Farmer, Ohio, in my brother Bill's 1949 Chevy when an older couple from New Jersey in a 1958 Buick and him collided head-on. The other couple survived.

This was one of the times in my life that I questioned the existence of God.

CHAPTER 3

My Life Was Turned Upside Down

*Do not be afraid or discouraged, for the
Lord your God will be with you.*

—Joshua 1:9

THE IMPACT THAT my father's death, at the age of thirty-nine, had on the family was profound. I personally was devastated and couldn't stop crying. For the next few days, the whole neighborhood supported us with their love and brought an abundance of foods to the house while sharing their sorrow with us. The funeral was held a few days later, and I remember, the church was filled to standing room only. Nearly all my classmates were there, and that meant the world to me. Dad's fellow workers were also there in abundance, along with our extended family and friends.

As we were leaving in the funeral limousine, I was bawling my eyes out, and I'll always remember what my grandfather Harry said to me, "Johnny, stop it right now. We will see him again someday."

We took the rest of the week off and tried returning to our old routine as much as possible. Here was my mom with five children, four of whom were still in school, and then having to support us all on social security. My older brother, Bill, had recently decided to join the air force, so it wouldn't be long until he would leave for enlistment.

As I returned to school for my sophomore year, having been elected president of our class, I entered this season of my life trying to maintain a positive attitude. I tried but just couldn't return to football due to the memory of my dad being there for me on parent's night.

So I went to work at a local gas station, owned by Cardinal Wolf, and saved enough money, $350, to buy my first car, a 1950 Robin Egg Blue convertible with a white top. Wow, I loved that car. It was so cool to drive, especially on warm days and starlit nights, with the top down. And girls—well, they seemed to really like it too.

One thing that was popular back then was to go cruising through a couple of nearby towns. There could be thirty to forty carloads of young people just following each other at a slow speed on a predetermined route for hours on end. When we were doing this, for some reason, a lot of girls would come out and walk on the streets for attention.

Another neat experience from that time was, there was a local dance show on Fort Wayne channel 15, hosted by a local icon by the name of Cactus Jack, and a bunch of classmates and I went and were on TV for this locally famous program. That was really a big deal for all of us, and we loved every moment of it.

John at age 16 with his first car

I loved driving my car to Cold Springs Resort at Hamilton, Indiana, on Saturday nights in the summertime for all the record hops. Everyone that thought they had a cool car would get there early and park out front in the first row. As I look back, my old Ford convertible probably didn't quite match up to the other cars in that row, but I loved it nonetheless.

It was about this same time that my mother met and started dating Jim Barnett from around the Greenville, Ohio area who had moved up to Sherwood, Ohio. I was not happy about this in any way, shape, or form. There was no one—and I mean no one—that could replace my dad.

He had a TV and appliance store in Sherwood, and my mom went to work for him. In later years, they moved to Port Richey, Florida, and opened a store.

I tended to hang out with both the good kids and sometimes the bad, as I wanted to be friends with everyone because of their great support for my family and me during these difficult times. I also went through my first puppy love scenario with a beautiful young girl by the name of Nancy Kinnison. That was quite the experience and was neat in many ways.

As the year progressed, I just could not focus on my studies, and I went from being an excellent student to being an average one.

My life consisted of my car, my friends, and starting to be mischievous in many ways. Without a father figure in my life, I, as a young teenager, just felt that I could do anything and everything that I wanted to do.

For example, a small group of us boys would go out and steal watermelon just for the fun of it. Another thing we loved to do was to go around the countryside and tip over outhouses. And like some other rebellious kids, I delved into a little drinking, fighting, hanging out at the local bars, shooting pool, and the like, all the while, during my junior and senior years, participating in basketball and track, acting in plays, and winning several dance contests.

Through my extracurricular activities, I sort of developed a reputation as a hot-tempered, fighting individual that was very competitive in all things. I just can't imagine what I had put my mother through in those days and some of the days that followed.

Going into my junior year, I had broken up with my previous girlfriend and started dating a wonderful young Christian girl in my class, Nancy Kimple.

Back then, if your date allowed you to hold her hand, that was a big step. And if it got to the point that she let you walk her to her parents' front door, and she kissed you good night, you thought you hit a home run.

Times really were different then as folks would leave their homes and didn't worry about locking them as we trusted one another. We even would leave the keys in our cars every time we got out of them, and the church doors and school doors were left unlocked. Nowadays, no one would consider doing that.

One memory is in the year 1961, after the junior-senior banquet, a group of us went to Columbia, Ohio, to one of our favorite hangouts, a burger place by the name of Jacks. We went there after ball games and almost anything that went on after school. I rode up that night with Larry DeWire in his grandmother's 1956 Chevrolet, which was a dark blue four-door sedan.

Roger Thorp and Glen Humphrey decided to ride along in the back seat. We just happened to be somewhere along the way to pick up a case of beer, which we put in the trunk of the car. After spending about an hour or so at Jacks, we decided to ride around for a while then head back to Edon. We were just talking, laughing, and having a great time.

The next thing I remember about that night was waking up in the hospital the next morning. A bunch of my classmates were in the room and outside, looking in the window.

It is then that I found out that Larry, the driver, and all of us had fallen to sleep as we were entering Edon, and we hit a concrete wall on the bridge that crosses Fish Creek going into town just past Russell Kuckuck's Shell station.

The car was completely totaled, and where I was sitting in the front seat on the passenger's side is where we took the brutal impact of that wall, pushing everything back to where I was sitting. God intervened. Amazingly, I came out of it with a few cuts and bruises, along with a badly injured right ankle. Everyone else was okay, but Glen had back issues from that day forward, and none of us were wearing seat belts.

At graduation, a couple of weeks later, when the junior class marched out to line up to welcome the graduating seniors, I was kind of a mess, with cuts on my face and a right ankle that was wrapped up. And I could only wear one shoe, which caused me to limp along the way. But I did it, and everything worked out.

During that summer, I worked again for the local farmers and was employed part-time at the Pure Gas station in town. I was very concerned about my ankle getting well enough to play basketball next year. Thankfully, it healed, and I got to play my favorite sport.

In our senior year, Kent Adams became our basketball coach, and we won the Williams County League Championship. I averaged around ten points per game, five rebounds, and three assists. One of my big attributes at 5'8" was that I could jump exceedingly high and could touch the rim with my wrist. Many times, I was asked to play against much taller players because of this.

In one game at Ashley, Indiana, as I was guarding a much taller player, and we went up for a rebound at the same time, he elbowed me in my mouth and knocked one of my front upper teeth out. My competitive spirit kicked in. Not wanting to be taken out of the game, as I ran past our bench, I just spit the tooth out to where coach Adams was standing.

All of this was before dunking was made legal and prior to the three-point line being established. As many of my shots were from far out, my scoring average would have been much higher if we would have had the three pointers back then.

When the Williams County tournament came up after the season, we were rated as one of the favorites. A couple of us got a little cocky and bleached our hair blond. Our first game was against a very good Montpelier team. And guess what, they blew us away by a huge score—so much for getting the big head. I think we learned a lot from that experience.

After the basketball season ended, I went back to my work routine and went through the motions of finishing school.

One custom back then was the seniors got to go on a senior trip to Washington, DC. I regretfully could not participate because of the financial position our family was in. A few weeks later, our graduation ceremony was upon us. I was excited in many ways but also somewhat concerned about what route I would be taking.

As the seniors lined up to march out, I had one male teacher walk up to me and say, "You shouldn't even be in this line." Wow! The first thought I had was, *I'll show you. Just watch!* The class of 1962 had in our four years of being together turned into one big happy family of lifelong friends.

Along the way, I had checked into information about a couple of small colleges that I might be able to play basketball for but, overall, just decided I couldn't afford to pursue that anymore and decided to go to work in a local factory.

CHAPTER 4

Going Out into the Adult World

*Your beginnings will seem humble, so
prosperous will your future be.*

—Job 8:7

THE FIRST THING I did was to go around to local factories and apply for a job. Bonnie worked at the Farmers & Merchants Bank in Montpelier, so one day I just rode with her, then walked to every factory in town, applying for work.

I got hired by a company by the name of Mohawk Tools, which was owned by the Hofbauer family. Frank, the patriot, was from Germany. This company manufactured cutting tools, drills, reamers, core drill, etc. My first job there was operating a flute grinding machine, which was a new concept, moving many tools from that procedure in the mill department to this one.

My starting wage was $2.87 per hour, and I started out on the day shift, and they were scheduled for ten-hour days, seven days a week. Well, so much for being a kid, I had to learn to grow up fast. During these long hours, there just wasn't much time for social activities.

The one reward for all of this is that I could go and buy a new car, a 1963 Chevy Impala for around $2,100.

For the first couple of years out of school and working full-time, trying to do the best I could, I rented an apartment and moved away from home. This was a big change in my life, but I felt it was necessary in the process of growing up! Buying my own groceries, paying the bills, and so forth. During this period of my life, I did a lot of things that the world says will make you happy.

> I have given them your word and the world has hated them, for they are not of the world any more than I am of the world. (John 17:14)

In this verse, Christ states, without question, that "they are not of the world." This is because He Himself is not of this world. This is a scripture that I certainly did not understand at the time.

Anyway, when I wasn't working, I drank some, shot a lot of pool, went to the racetracks at Bryan Motor Speedway and Butler Motor Speedway. My family had been involved in racing for many years, starting with my uncle John, dads' brother, who owned a number fifty-seven stock cars. When I was about twelve years old, on a night when his regular driver was not there, my dad jumped in the car without us knowing it and raced.

I regularly attended the Cold Springs Resort Saturday night dances at Hamilton Lake and did some dancing. These dances drew around three thousand kids from the local and surrounding communities. Normally, a DJ from WOWO radio in Fort Wayne, Indiana, emceed these events. I also had a temper and seemed to spend a lot of time getting into fist fights. It seemed like every night at the dance, someone from somewhere would end up going outside to settle a dispute.

And amazingly, a lot of times it was me. I even ended up in the Steuben County Jail one night after such and occasion. This was probably where my reputation as a fighter grew as I never lost a fight.

One night, at Cold Springs, I asked a girl to dance that I thought was someone else, and it turned out to be Pat Hug from Blakeslee, who attended Edon High School. She was from what I considered a prominent Catholic family of ten children, whose father was a big grain and hog farmer that sat on the board of directors at the Edon State Bank and on the Edon Northwest School Board.

Coming from a poorer lifestyle, I felt a little apprehensive about being with Pat on the dance floor or anywhere else for that matter. As was a custom back then, I asked her if I could drive her home after the dance. She said, "Let me check with my sister and see." I took her home that night, and we started dating.

Work at Mohawk was going very well, and I eventually became a lead person on my shift. We were still working a lot of hours, but I was finally getting some weekends off. This gave me a chance to start enjoying life outside of work.

In the summer of 1964, Pat and I continued to date off and on. One thing I remember is when we would return after a date, her mother, Muriel, would almost always bring me out a treat to the car, which normally consisted of fresh-baked cookies.

We both had things we enjoyed doing with each other and sometimes without. We very often would go our own ways and then cross paths occasionally. One day, in late August, she called me and asked if we could meet and talk.

We agreed that I would go to Mose Moore's house, where she was spending a lot of time babysitting. This family was a stronghold in Blakeslee, Ohio, as his father was Sam, who started historical Sam's Place, which Mose still ran.

Pat and I hadn't been together for a couple of months, so I was wondering what in the world she wanted to talk about. Throughout our relationship, I felt that I was truly in love with her, and it hurt every time we decided to go our own way. I lived in Montpelier at the time, so on the drive over, I started to get a little anxious about it all. Upon arrival, the Moore family had gone somewhere. I knocked on the door, and she answered and invited me in.

We sat down on the couch and carried on a short "nice to see you type conversation" when all at once she broke down in tears and told me she was pregnant.

I was somewhat shocked and thought, *Man, I've got to let this sink in.* After a few days, we decided that we had to break the news to our families and then set a date to get married.

CHAPTER 5

Becoming a Father

Train up a child in the way he should go, even when he is old, he will not depart from it.

—Proverbs 22:6

THE THOUGHT OF being a husband and father sank in rather quickly with me, realizing this meant that I now had a family to take care of.

We got married on September 26, 1964, in the Catholic Church in Blakeslee in the parsonage, with our parents being present and another schoolmate, who became one of my best friends, standing in as best man. Bruce "Stook" Stonestreet and I hung out together a lot.

He lived on a farm north of Edon, and his father, William Stonestreet, owned some gravel pits up by Angola, Indiana. Much of the gravel from theses pits was used in the building of the Indiana–Ohio turnpike back in the midfifties. There were many times Stook would ask me to come up and spend the night in our grade-school years, and we got to know each other very well.

After the wedding, we went on a short weekend honeymoon, staying overnight in Angola, Indiana, on Saturday, then in Quincy, Michigan, on Sunday night. The next thing we did was rent an upstairs apartment on Jonesville Street in Montpelier, Ohio, from Mr. and Mrs. Long so I would be close to work. The rent back then for a large two-bedroom apartment was $50 per month. Then I sold my 1963 Impala and bought a 1956 four-door Bel Air to improve our finances and expenses.

As was tradition then, when you married a Catholic, you became a Catholic. I had many friends from school that were from Blakeslee and attended church there, so I felt comfortable with the transition. I took some classes about Catholicism and became a part of the Knights of Columbus. Then I started doing things as required, including going to confession periodically.

As time proceeded, we got into a regular routine of husband and wife—me going to work every day and Pat maintaining the household.

She was a pretty good cook and an excellent housekeeper with everything being perfectly clean and always in place. I believe she inherited all of this from her mother, Muriel.

John Winright—The new foreman at Mohawk Tools - 09-23-1964

Then one day at work, I was called into the office of Henry Hutchens, the manufacturing superintendent, and he greeted me and then told me they were looking for a supervisor to take over the night shift operations. He asked me if I would be interested. I was somewhat shocked as I was only twenty years old, and there were guys that had been there much longer than me. He explained that it would be a salaried position and an integral part of management. I told him, "Absolutely," and everything proceeded from there.

On April 6, 1965, Pat went into labor and delivered a baby boy that we named Tobias Lee Winright. I was now a father and had that additional responsibility. The thought of being a husband and father sank in rather quickly with me, realizing this meant I now had a family to take care of. The joy of seeing a baby that was yours for the first time and realizing the reality of being his father was amazing.

Shortly after our son's birth, we looked at and purchased our first home in the Hillcrest subdivision across Route 20 and the Hillcrest Golf Course. It was a two-story home built into the side of a hill. In 1965, this home sold for $18,000, and our payment ended up being a little over $100 per month. I was hoping that I would be able to make that monthly payment.

Over the years, I had known and had my haircut by Joe Mohre in Blakeslee. Joe had recently gotten his real estate broker's license, and I approached him about going to work for him as a salesman.

He told me that would be great and then gave me a book to study before going to Columbus to take a state exam. I studied whenever I got a chance and then a few weeks later went for my exam, passed, and became Joe's first salesman at Joe Mohre's Real Estate Company.

I continued working at Mohawk and selling real estate on a part-time basis. After making a few sales, I felt much more comfortable about the house payment being covered. I loved being in the real estate business and soon thought about doing some investing in rental properties. I received another promotion at Mohawk becoming the maintenance superintendent over every aspect of the company. Of course, along with this came another increase in my wages.

Between 1965 to 1970, we were blessed with three more sons—Timothy John, Troy Thomas, and Tyler Clinton—all of whom were very special in their own ways. Family time was awesome, and we did all the things required to be one big happy family. We invested in several rental properties with one of the first being a four-unit building. We ended up with a total of eleven rentals.

As I looked back over my life, I was very proud of what we had accomplished!

CHAPTER 6

Hard Work and Dedication Can Bring Rewards

Pride goes before destruction, and a haughty spirit before the fall.

—Proverbs 16:18 KJV

IT WAS AT this time in 1970 that I was told the Stonestreet farm that was mentioned in an earlier chapter was for sale. Bruce's dad, William, had passed away and his mother, Minnie, was going to move to a cottage she had at Hamilton Lake.

We had been talking for a while about how it would be nice to raise the boys in the country like we both had been raised. So I decided to go and talk to Minnie.

As we met and talked, it seemed that Minnie was very excited that she might be able to sell the farm to a close friend of Bruce's.

She then gave me a price of $20,000 and said that she would prefer to sell it on a contract rather than having it financed by a bank. So we discussed the details, and I told her that I would like to discuss it with Pat and get with her soon.

Farms at that time were selling for around $300 per acre, including the buildings, so the price of $500 per acre did seem a little high. Our house was appraised at about the same amount, which was a little more than we gave for it a few years earlier.

After discussing it with Pat, we decided that was the route that we would like to go. So I got back with Minnie and told her that we would like to proceed but would have to sell our house first. She said that was fine. Amazingly, we had ours sold within weeks and proceeded with the purchase and move. Almost immediately, I heard stories of people all around saying we were crazy for giving so much for that farm.

I just took what was being said as a grain of salt and moved on with our life. The intersection where the farm was located had been known as Stonestreet Corners for many years.

What excitement filled the air as we moved on to this new adventure with our boys. They would be attending the same schools that their mother and I had with the sons and daughters of many of our friends and acquaintances. The house was one of many memories from when I was a kid hanging out with Bruce "Stook" Stonestreet. I could even remember his dad, William, sitting in the living room on Saturday nights, watching wrestling every week, and Minnie fixing meals for the family in the kitchen as now we were there doing some of the same things with our boys.

We bought a couple of horses for the boys and a dog. We had a beautiful space for a garden and all this land, along with a few acres of woods. The Best family lived just east of us, and their kids and ours became good friends and spent a lot of time playing together.

I felt so good and excited about how all our hard work had paid off and looked forward to what the future held for us. I visualized many happy years ahead with a wife that I loved and four sons that I could watch mature and grow in many ways and as they followed in my father Clinton's and my footsteps, watch them participate in sports.

Since my father-in-law was a big farmer, he agreed that he would farm our place on shares, where we split both the cost and the profit of the crops that came off the land. I loved every aspect of our lives at that time. We had a few fences that he suggested we remove, so Pat, the boys, and I all made that a project for a couple of weeks until it was completed.

ONLY BELIEVE AND NEVER GIVE UP

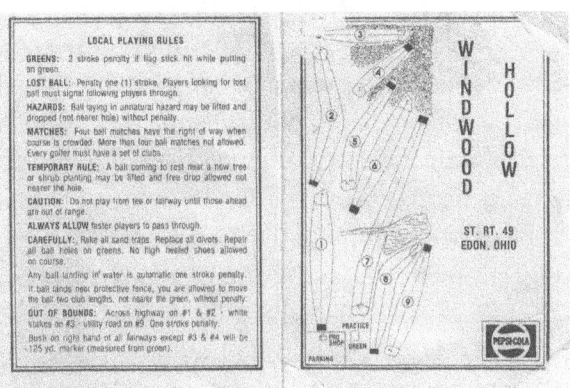

Windwood Hollow Golf Course play card

About three years later, a thought came to my mind about building a golf course on our property. The more I thought about it, the more intriguing it became. I golfed periodically but was really never all that good at it.

My father-in-law and other friends and I would go around to different courses periodically and play, and we all did have a lot of fun—for me, mostly from a fellowship standpoint. So if I built a course, it would be strictly from an investment standpoint for me.

I discussed it with Pat, and she didn't seem to really have an opinion on it one way or the other, so I proceeded to investigate everything further.

I contacted a person in Toledo, Ohio, who designed courses and had him see what he could come up with. A few weeks later, we met, and he had drawings on a forty-acre, nine-hole, thirty-five parcourse. He didn't even charge me for it and let me take it home with me. Over the next few days, I made a few changes on it and then thought about how I should proceed from there.

The next thing I did was research sources for irrigation systems, grass seed, and everything else that would be required. A gentleman called me and set up an appointment to come and discuss all this with me. He was an amazing help and had a lot of experience in the process of building golf courses and offered to advise and supervise the whole construction process with me at no cost if I bought everything that was needed through his company.

This all took place in 1973, and the three older boys were all in school. And Pat decided that she wanted to go to work on the turnpike as a toll collector, while our neighbor Dianne Best, who had become very good friends with Pat, would babysit Tyler until he started school. I didn't really like the idea because I was always used to being the lone provider, but I told her to go ahead if that's really what she wanted to do.

As things progressed, I got a quote on what the course would cost: $100,000. Back then, that was a lot of money. One thing that helped is that the farm was paid off, so I went to the Edon State Bank to discuss further. Upon looking at the drawings and discussing in detail, I went ahead and applied for the loan. A few days later, it came back approved. Wow, it was time to make a final decision.

Then I contacted two very close friends—Andy Nixon, a local contractor, and Roy Rozell, a local landscaper—to see if we could coordinate everything with my consultant and then to make this all happen. It took a few weeks, but everything fell into place. It was decided, as we proceeded, that we would turn our barn into a clubhouse for the course.

So now it was time to make a final decision, whether to start right away or wait until the following year. One part of that decision was the fact that we had a beginning crop of soybeans and corn covering the acreage.

The original Windwood Hollow clubhouse

We really had no idea about how long the complete project would take. And now that we had everything in place, I was eager to get moving on it. So that is what we did, even though it meant tearing up the crops that had been planted. Many folks expressed a concern for that decision, but it was mine to make, so I did it. Construction began on Windwood Hollow Golf Course, and it was completed in late 1974, when we opened for a few weeks late in the season. Our official opening was in April of 1975.

During this whole process of working full-time in a factory, selling real estate part-time, and focusing on this investment, something else was taking place.

CHAPTER 7

A Devastating Time in My Personal Life

> The Lord is near to those who have a broken heart
> and saves such as have a contrite spirit.
>
> —Psalm 34:18

IN THE FALL of 1975, I came home from work one evening, and the boys were all setting around our Walton-type table in the kitchen, eating supper, when I walked through the door. I said hi to them all as I normally did, but I just sensed something different in the atmosphere.

Then their mother came into the kitchen, crying. I asked her what the matter was, and she told me she would tell me after the boys were done eating and when they went outside. Well, a few minutes later, when the boys were finished and exited the kitchen, she told me, "I no longer want to be married to you and want a divorce."

This was another time that I questioned whether there was a God or not.

I was absolutely caught off guard and devastated by what I was hearing. Details were discussed at greater length, and I do not feel comfortable talking about them here. But as I look back, I must share part of the blame. For one, I was always a very jealous husband and always focusing on being a good provider, working a lot of hours to succeed, and focusing on things rather than my loved ones a lot of the time. I moved out of the house into a house trailer in the Edon trailer court. I just could not believe how everything had transpired to the point it had.

Well, as time progressed, we were divorced on Valentines Day, Friday, February 14, 1975! I had visitation with the boys every other weekend, and in between was the most lonesome that I had ever been in my life. To cover that lonesomeness, I would spend a lot of time in bars, trying to drown my feelings. But I still maintained my work ethic and schedule.

I felt like a total failure at this point in my life, wondering why and how I was not good enough for her. So many thoughts and insecurities crept upon me, and I just did not know what to do as I spent hours in sadness and tears.

I was absolutely devastated and felt I had no way to turn or anywhere to go forward with my life. One night, after being in Toledo and drinking, as I was heading back home, the thought entered my mind that I just didn't want to go on living. I was driving a 1964 Corvette that I had recently bought that was a very fast car with a huge engine.

As I was nearing Delta, Ohio, I was coming upon an elevated railroad that, as you went under it, were huge concrete retaining wall on both sides. I pressed down on the accelerator all the way to the floor and was focused on turning and hitting the one on the left as I came up to it. For some reason, no matter how hard I tried with all my strength, the wheel just would not turn. Guardian angels?

As I got to the other side, I pulled off the road and cried, asking why. Several years later, I received the answer: "God had a plan for your life."

I did some dating but just couldn't allow myself to be serious with anyone because I still wasn't over my feelings for Pat. I just could not let go of the life I had lived and loved for the previous eleven years.

As far as work was concerned, I decided I needed a change of atmosphere, so I left Mohawk and went to work for a company by the name of Kustom Fit in Pioneer, Ohio, as a supervisor. It was definitely a big change, and quite honestly, I really did not like it that well.

About this same time, Pat decided to move to Florida with the boys after selling her half of Windwood Hollow to her father and brother. This was another real setback as I would not be seeing my boys on a regular basis.

The one advantage was that I could move back into the house at the course. Being single and alone after those years of family life was a real challenge for me. I sought out many of the things of this world to try to find peace and happiness, including buying a new Corvette. But nothing worked as my life was shattered.

One night, after I had moved back in, there was a knock on the door, and when I answered, it was the pastor from the church down the road. He came in and almost immediately started sharing with me about God and how he could help me. I stood up and told him to get out of my house because there could not be a God for these things to be happening in my life. Every time I think about this now, I am totally embarrassed by it.

Then an opportunity came up at work that was very appealing to me. The owner of Kustom Fit bought a yacht company that built Mariner Yachts that were manufactured in Taiwan. These yachts ranged in size from twenty-four feet all the way up to fifty feet in length and had an excessive amount of teak wood in them.

Rich Cooley, the head of HR who knew Pat had moved to Florida with the boys, came and asked me if I would be willing to take three or four boats down to Florida that we could take potential buyers on sea trials in. It didn't take me long to say, "Yes, I will do that."

The location we chose was Tarpon Springs, Florida, which was about twenty miles north of Clearwater, where Pat and the boys were and about six miles west of Port Richey, where my mom and Jim lived, along with my brother Tom.

CHAPTER 8

A New Beginning

> Forget the former things; do not dwell on the past. See, I am doing a new thing!
>
> —Isaiah 43:18–19:

ON THE WAY down, I was asked by my company to go to Annapolis, Maryland, for a big boat show they were participating in, so I did and learned a lot about what our boats were like and about the industry. This was a great experience, and Annapolis was beautiful. We even went sailing on Chesapeake Bay, which was a fantastic event on its own.

From there, I drove on down to Florida and rented an apartment beside the bayou in Tarpon Springs. Then we got three yachts transported and put into the water to be docked at the local marina on the river that led out to the Gulf of Mexico. We put another one right down town at a dock beside the famous Pappas Restaurant that, at that time, served around three thousand folks per day. It was a Greek restaurant and served a great Greek salad, along with fantastic food.

I went there on a regular basis and got to know the owners well. It turned out that they had an annual cookout and get together at a ranch they owned and invited the governor and other important people to attend. I was amazed when they extended an invitation to me to participate too. Who was I but a little country boy from Ohio? I accepted and went and had a great time as I was treated like a special guest, just like everyone else.

I was in my midthirties, and part of what I had to do was maintain the boats on a regular basis. The teak wood had to be treated in an ongoing basis. I loved just wearing a swimsuit most of the day doing these duties, thus inheriting a great tan.

Along with my long hair and Fu Manchu mustache, I thought that I was cool. A lot of people walked by our dock every day as I was hanging out on the boat. It sure was a big change from where I grew up in little Edon, Ohio.

One of the main challenges was that I had to be prepared to take potential buyers on trial cruises in the boat of their choice. I had never sailed a boat before in my whole life. The biggest boat that I had ever maneuvered was probably an eight-foot rowboat on some small lakes back up North. Now twenty-four- to-fifty-four-foot sailboats in the Gulf of Mexico?

On top of that, I had to teach myself, without any navigational equipment being installed until after the boats were sold to find my way out into the Gulf of Mexico and back to the boat docks on each trial run. About this same time, I moved out of my apartment and onto the fifty-four-footer. Thankfully, Rich Cooley, the HR person from Kustom Fit, was my boss now, and he came down to spend a few days so that we could go out into the Gulf and teach ourselves as much as we could about sailing.

I started to feel more confident in motoring our way out into the deeper waters and then hoisting the sales up on the masts and letting the wind propel us through the waters. I was starting to fall in love with the world of sailing.

Whenever I could, I would drive around the community, getting to know and appreciate this new environment I was in. It was 75 percent Greek, with sponge docks, fishing excursions, and everything—beautiful bayous, beaches, and tourist everywhere. I was able to see my sons on a regular basis once again, and things were starting to settle down some in my life.

In my drives, for some reason, a small Assembly of God Church drew my attention every time I drove by it. It did not even look like it was open, but the sign in front stated the times of services.

I was still seeking happiness in my life by focusing on the things of this world: alcohol, dating, pornography, smoking (pipes and cigars), material possessions—the things that we think will bring joy to our lives. I kept functioning as well as I could day to day and taking customers out on sea trial runs in the yachts periodically. These people came from all around the country.

But every time I drove by that little church, something kept drawing me to it. Having been raised in the Lutheran Church and then being Catholic for eleven years, I just didn't understand why.

One Sunday morning, after a night out on the town, I woke up early and couldn't get that church off my mind. I remembered that the sign said that the services started at 10:00 a.m., and I certainly had plenty of time to get around and go. I kept fighting that urge until about 9:00 a.m. and then thought, *What the heck. Why not!*

CHAPTER 9

A Life-Changing Experience

> Therefore, if anyone is in Christ, he is a new creation; old things have passed away; behold, all things have become new.
>
> —2 Corinthians 5:17

AS I PULLED into the parking lot that morning, anticipation set in to the point where I almost backed out and went home. I sat in my car, smoking on a big, old cigar and still carrying a little bit of a hangover from the night before. It was the beginning of February and a nice cool crisp morning in Florida but still sunshiny! I saw a few people pulling in and finally thought, *Well, here goes* and exited my car and headed that way.

As I entered the church, I was welcomed by several folks that had big smiles on their faces and just acted different as they let their love flow. I am sure there was a stench on me of alcohol and tobacco, but that didn't seem to matter to these folks. I was aching to be loved at the time because of what I had gone through in my life. As the service started, Pastor Paul Hale came out and welcomed everyone. Then they went into a worship service like nothing I had ever experienced before. I had never seen so much enthusiasm and excitement in church my whole life. They even raised their hands and voices in praise to God.

Then Pastor Hale gave the message that God had laid on his heart. One thing that stood out was he read John 3:16: "For God so loved the world that He gave His only begotten Son, that whoever believes in Him should not perish but have everlasting life." And at the end of his message, he gave what he called an altar call.

This was all totally new to me, and then a lady started speaking in a foreign language out loud, like she was praying. I just assumed that she was praying in Greek as that was what most of the community was made up of. After the service, several folks came up and told me they were so happy to see me there.

One gentleman asked me what I thought of the service. I told him that it was different but that I enjoyed it. I told him, even the lady praying out loud in Greek was neat. He kind of smiled and said, "Oh no, that was her speaking in tongues."

My response to this was, "You mean this is a Holy Roller church," to which he laughed and said, "Well, I guess you could say that."

As I was leaving, I thought, *Wow, as kids growing up, we had always made fun of and joked about Holy Rollers,* and here, I was leaving a service in their church that I enjoyed.

During the next couple of days, I could not stop thinking about that church, the Tarpon Springs Assembly of God, and went back for every service for a couple of weeks. Then on a Sunday night on February 24, 1980, I walked up from the back of the church during altar call and accepted Jesus Christ as my personal Lord and Savior. I knew right then that I would never question God's existence again.

> Therefore, if anyone is in Christ, he is a new creation; old things have passed away; behold, all things have become new. (2 Corinthians 5:17 NKJV)

I went home after church that night as a changed person. If someone sincerely asks for God's forgiveness and invites Him into our life, we will be changed. The very first thing I did when I got home was to throw away all pornography, cigars, pipes and tobaccos, and anything else that was there that I did not want in my life anymore. I was a new creation.

I just couldn't believe that God loved a sinner like me so much that He would allow His Son to die on the cross for me.

As the next few days passed by, I just could not put my Bible down. For some reason, I was led to the book of Psalms first, then to Proverbs. Following that, I went to the New Testament from Matthew through Revelation. I just could not get enough of God's word. Every time the church doors were open, I was there. And sometimes when they weren't open, I would still go and sit in the parking lot, reflecting on what God was doing in my life.

One of the hymns that we sang in church kept coming into my mind, "Blessed Assurance, Jesus Is Mine," and I would sing it constantly.

Another thing the Holy Spirit told me to do was to write a couple of letters, asking for forgiveness from a couple of people from my past. The first one that I wrote was to a man by the name of Rell Myers, whom I had worked with at Mohawk. Rell was a very strong Christian and never hid it in any way.

I was the contrary and quite ornery one, constantly and intentionally swearing in front of him using the Lord's name in vain, joked about his religion, and made fun of him. This man never showed any animosity toward me. I couldn't wait to get my letter of apology in the mail to him and share that I was a born-again Christian now.

The other one I wrote included a reimbursement for some money that I had stolen while in school. A couple of friends and I that were on the basketball team together stayed and hid in the school after basketball practice one night, and after everyone had departed, we went into the cafeteria and stole some money out of their cashbox and then went downtown and splurged on some treats. Kent Adams, who was our basketball coach back then, was now the superintendent, so I mailed a letter of apology to him, along with what I thought was the full amount of money taken that night. I explained to him that I had recently accepted the Lord as my Savior and was a new creation.

I wanted to tell everyone what I saw about Jesus! A few days later, Rich Cooley was scheduled to come down to meet with some people from New Jersey that he had scheduled to come for a trial run out into the Gulf of Mexico on our twenty-four-foot yacht. I had to pick him up at the Tampa airport, and as we were driving back to Tarpon Springs and talking, he suddenly stopped the conversation and said very seriously, "What is going on with you? You are totally different than the John Winright I have always known."

I told him, "Rich, I have accepted Jesus as my Lord and Savior."

He said, "What?"

So I repeated myself then proceeded to tell him how everything had changed. I said, "The flowers looked and smelled more beautiful. The sunrises and sunsets were more prominent than ever before, and I now have a joy that I have never experienced before in my life."

CHAPTER 10

Only Believe, and Never Give Up

> Be of good courage, and he shall strengthen
> your heart, all ye that hope in the Lord.
>
> —Psalm 31:24

THE NEXT DAY, we were scheduled for the trial run out into the Gulf with Rich's clients.

As we met at the marina for departure around midafternoon, we greeted and welcomed one another and boarded for departure. It was a beautiful sunny afternoon with a nice breeze to help us in this sailing adventure. As we got about a mile out, we lifted the sails up on the masts and let the wind take us on our journey.

The winds increased and decreased throughout the day, which created situations for adjustments, which the clients needed to see and were very thankful for. Finally, it was time to head back to the marina. But as we got closer to our destination, a fog started settling in. As I stated earlier, these boats had no instrumentation installed yet, so everything was determined by landmarks and the naked eye. Just as I saw the first buoy at the entrance off in the distance, it immediately disappeared in the fog.

We all looked at each other and said, "What do we do now?" The immediate answer was to weigh anchor until the fog lifted, which we all knew could be hours, so that is what we did. As we set there, I recalled in my mind some of the things I had been hearing and learning in church. Two of which were pray and step out in faith, believing.

After a short period of waiting, Rich, being frustrated, said, "What are we going to do?"

That is when I shared that "I believe we should pray and ask God for His help."

Rich and the couple with us kind of snickered and said, "Whatever."

So we bowed our heads, and I asked God for His help and deliverance from the circumstances we were facing.

Channel markers are navigational aids that mark safe passage for ships and boats through channels and waterways. They typically consist of buoys or beacons, colored and numbered or lettered to indicate the direction and side of the channel.

These markers help prevent vessels from running aground or colliding with underwater hazards. As I said earlier, I saw the first one, and then it disappeared in the fog.

After we prayed within minutes, I looked up and saw the first buoy that I had seen earlier, even though the fog was still thick all around us and everything else. I told Rich, "Let's weigh anchor and head that way."

He said, "Are you serious?"

I said, "Yes, I believe God is answering our prayer." This being the first time since I said the sinner's prayer in faith, it was a test that I was being obedient to.

As we proceeded toward the marker and passed it, the next one came into view. But as we turned and looked back, the first one was no longer visible, and the fog was still dense all around us. As we passed the second one, the same scenarios happened.

The one we just passed disappeared, and the next one came into sight. This happened all the way back to the marina and our dock, and we eventually were tied up and safe.

Rich and the guests said, "I don't know what just happened, but we'll take it."

I told them that God just answered our prayer. This was the second miracle that I got to see God perform in my life from prayer and faith and believing! The first one was my prayer of salvation being answered.

As time went by, we were having difficulty in selling the yachts because of the economy and high interest rates. A decision was made to decrease the sales facilities around the country, including the one in Florida.

I had become very close to an older gentleman at church by the name of Wilford West, who owned a local lumber company, truss plant, and manufactured home business, along with Robert D'Andrea, who owned the local Christian TV network CTN on channel 22 in Tampa and then in Largo.

When he heard of my dilemma, he asked if I had a résumé. I told him that I did, and he asked if I could bring it with me to his office and meet with him.

I said, "Sure," and we set a date and time. Upon meeting, Wilford was very impressed with my résumé and offered me a job as general manager of their truss and manufactured home facility, which was out in the country in the middle of nowhere. I eagerly told him, "Yes, I would accept." So another chapter in my life, jobwise, would begin.

This was an amazing experience learning a new industry and working for a Christian organization. Wilford and I would meet every morning at 4:00 or 5:00 a.m. to discuss the day ahead and then move forward. The plant that I ran manufactured roof trusses and stick built homes that we would deliver to the construction sites.

Most of the employees were what we called Florida crackers country folks for sure. One day, one of them came into my office with a burlap bag and said he had something he wanted to show me.

As he opened it, I was shocked to see it full of rattlesnakes. He laughed and walked out the door. I found out later that it was a hobby of theirs to catch these snakes and then sell them to some local universities for studies.

A couple of weeks later, I was invited to attend a church service at one of their churches away, out in the middle of nowhere on an old gravel road. As I drove there, I thought about the Bible verse *"Behold, I have given you authority to tread on serpents and scorpions, and over all the power of the enemy, and nothing shall hurt you" (Luke 10:19).* I was thinking, *What if they were one of those churches that had snakes?* I got there, and they had a fantastic spirit-filled service, with no snakes.

About this same time, my oldest son, Toby, came to live with me. We found a little cottage at Chrystal Beach, close to the worship leader, Bob Chambers, from our home church. He had a son, Steve, that became a very good friend of Toby's.

Toby attended church with me and became very involved in everything, especially the youth program. This was a very neat time in my life, and I was enjoying every minute of it.

When fall came, we had to move from the little cottage because they had it rented out for the winter to someone from up North, so we found a two-bedroom condo in Tarpon Springs, close to the entrance of beautiful Howard Park.

Another decision I made during this period of my life was to go ahead and sell my half of Windwood Hollow golf course to my former brother-in-law and father-in-law.

One day, while reading the Tampa *Tribune* newspaper, I saw in the help wanted section a job for a general manager of a company out of Buffalo, New York, that was starting a new division in Pinellas Park, Florida, which was close by. I thought about that and prayed for a few days, then gave them a call to set up an interview.

They acted very interested in speaking to me, so we set up a meeting with Paul Harder, the president, and Leon Segal, VP of sales, who represented the company, Bufkor of Buffalo, New York. A few days passed, and they called me back and offered me the job, which paid substantially more than my present one.

The year that all of this happened was 1980, four years after my divorce. My life was finally getting on track; thanks to my transformation to being a child of God.

CHAPTER 11

A New Season in My Life

To everything there is a season, A time for every purpose under heaven.

—Ecclesiastes 3:1

UPON MY STARTING date, the first thing I had to do was to fly to Buffalo, New York, to view their facilities and to get an understanding of their product. They manufactured jewelry displays and packaging or jewelry boxes. This was quite different than my background in cutting tools, drills, and reamers at Mohawk.

I was amazed when I found out that it was a multi-million-dollar business. Flying to a large city and staying at a large Marriott Hotel was a somewhat intimidating experience for this country boy.

The company was founded in 1895 by the Korn family and William, Irving, and Morton Korn were still operating the company that had been handed down to them over the years. This was my first experience to know and work for a classical Jewish family. I found them to be great people with fantastic business minds. The manufacturing of the displays was mostly done by hand, very few machines involved.

When not at the factory, Paul Harder spent time with me, showing me the city. One night, he invited me to his house for supper. He lived in a small town out in the suburbs by the name of Eden, New York. I thought, *What a coincidence*, since I was from Edon, Ohio.

On my last night before leaving, the Korns took me out to dinner, and to my surprise, Goldie Hawn, the actress who was in town doing a movie with Burt Reynolds, was sitting at a table right beside us. When I returned home, I told everyone that I ate dinner with Goldie Hawn on my last night in Buffalo.

After this trip, and once I returned to Florida, the next scenario was to get our facility in Pinellas Park set up for manufacturing. The company sent a gentleman by the name of Ralph down to stay and help until this project was completed. The next step was for me to fly to San Diego, California, to a division out there, Bufkor Pacific, to be trained by Carl and Doris Balducci, the GMs. I stayed at the historic St. Francis Hotel right downtown, close to the world-famous Warf. What an experience for this farm boy.

I had heard about things in the city and California but never really seen them—people eating out of garbage cans; gays walking the streets, holding hands; prostitutes everywhere at night; also, street evangelist all over the city.

Being a new Christian, I was really impressed with this and loved watching them preach. I stayed in San Fransisco for a little over a week, then returned home.

Once there, my responsibility was to hire everyone that we needed to start up the operation. The first thing I did was to call back to Ohio and ask Jack Stiverson, who was a supervisor at Kustom Fit, if he and his wife, Sandy, would be interested in coming down and running our production on the floor. It took a few days, but he called me back and said they would. They arrived just a couple of weeks later.

Things started moving fast as we started to receive orders for production. Jack asked me about contacting another Kustom Fit employee by the name of Pete Leaders to come down and run our shipping department. We contacted him, and he said yes.

From there, I proceeded to hire people to fill all manufacturing and office positions, and things filled up quickly. Before we knew it, we were producing and shipping jewelry displays all around the country.

My personal life now was taken up by my church, work, and family, and this all kept me busy. I continued to attend church every time the doors were open, stayed in the word of God and prayer, and progressed daily in my walk with Him. I loved spending time with my sons Toby, Tim, Troy, and Tyler, and seeing them grow and play sports.

Two places that I wanted to visit were PTL to see their duplicate of the upper room and Jimmy Swaggert's campus in Baton Rouge, Louisiana. Through my travels, the opportunity for these visits were realized, and I enjoyed both tremendously. The upper room touched me very heavily, and it has stuck in my spirit ever since.

CHAPTER 12

God Had a Plan for My Happiness to Return to My Life

> Take delight in the Lord, and he will give
> you the desires of your heart.
>
> —Psalm 37:4

IT HAD BEEN six years since my divorce was final. I had dated quite a few different ladies over these years but just couldn't allow myself to get serious with any of them for fear of being hurt again. But down deep inside, I was hoping that would change, and someday I could be in a happy relationship once again that would turn into a happy marriage.

    The company kept growing, and as it did, we continued to hire more people. As stated earlier, I did everything, including all the hiring. One day in March of 1981, my secretary waked into my office and laid an application on my desk and told me that they were here for their interview. I told her to send them on back to my office. An attractive young lady by the name of Marilyn Fetter entered the door, and I told her to have a seat so we could talk.

    She had moved down to Pinellas Park from Columbus, Indiana. After discussing the job with her, we went out for a tour of the shop and introduced her to some of the crew. She then went back into the office to fill out the proper paperwork and started the next week.

During the next few months, I made a couple of trips up to the corporate offices in Buffalo, New York, and then out to San Francisco, California, at Bufkor Pacific to see how things were going. Along with that, I did everything daily that had to be done at our plant, Bufkor South.

My office had a window behind my desk that I could look out of and see the process of manufacturing going on, but I also enjoyed going out on the floor on a regular basis and seeing everything as it progressed through the different departments from the beginning in the wood room to being covered in various fabrics consisting of different textures and colors, to the shipping of everything.

I enjoyed speaking to everyone as I walked through but found that I did stop and talk to some individuals more than others.

Well, as you've probably already guessed, Marilyn Fetter just happened to be one of those. Working with different colors daily, I asked her what her favorite color was, and she said red. Back then, I dressed daily in suit pants with a sports coat and a knit shirt. Well, for some crazy reason I was led to wear a red shirt under my sports coat the next day.

As time passed, the more we talked, the more we seemed to have in common. Finally, I asked her if she would like to go out to dinner sometime. She said yes, so we set a date for the following Friday night to go and eat at a place called Pier One in Saint Petersburg. We sat there for a couple of hours and talked.

I found out that she was the daughter of Eugene and Martha Hitch, who were originally from Kentucky, and that she had two brothers and three sisters.

She went into some more detail, and it was all very interesting to me. I also shared a lot about my family and everything that I could about my life. One of the biggest things that came out of the conversation and something I was somewhat concerned about was our age difference, with her being thirteen years younger than me. My oldest son was only eight years younger than her!

During the evening, I shared with her more about my walk with Christ and that one thing I would never give up to anyone was the relationship that I had with Him. If I remember correctly, that struck her in a positive way and not a negative one. I then asked her if she would like to come to church with me sometime. She said, "Sure!"

Back then, in the Assembly of God Church, folks dressed up, with men in suits and ties and women in very conservative dresses. They were very careful about appearances. Well, the morning came that Marilyn attended her first service with me. When I picked her up, she was dressed in a halter top and jeans. My first thought was, should I tell her to go back and change? But then I thought, *Maybe she doesn't have anything else to wear.* So we went on to the service, and everyone made her feel welcome, and she seemed to enjoy the experience. The following week, when I picked her up for church, she was dressed in a much more conservative manner.

Marilyn's parents, Martha Dimple and Eugene Hitch

One thing about her family was that they were very talented. Her dad could play the guitar, banjo, harmonica, and any other instrument he laid his hands on. Marilyn was the only child of the six to learn to play the guitar. Eugene had sung and played on a radio station in Adair County, Kentucky, before he and Martha married.

At the age of sixteen, Marilyn had become the lead female vocalist in a small country band that performed at local bars, as well as VHWs in Columbus and the surrounding area. One opportunity the band had was to sing in Nashville, Indiana, at the Little Opry House, the same venue as Bill Monroe, a well-known bluegrass singer. Marilyn's mother, Martha, and older sister, Betty, were also blessed with beautiful voices.

A few weeks later, I shared with Pastor Hale about Marilyn's talents as a guitar player and singer and asked if she could do a special some Sunday morning. He responded by saying, "Sure." So we set it up for the following Sunday.

As I share this, I get a little choked up because that morning, during the service, it came time for her special, so she proceeded to walked up front, picked her guitar up, and sang one of the most beautiful presentations of "Amazing Grace" that I had ever heard. When she finished, everyone in the congregation broke out in applause.

It wasn't long after that when we both joined the choir and sang in every service with them. Our worship leader was Bob Chambers, who couldn't really carry a tune but was one of the greatest and most inspirational worship leaders that I have ever seen.

As far as our personal relationship, it kept growing stronger. We had discussed Marilyn moving into the condo with Toby and I off and on because she was going to need a place to go soon.

I still wasn't sure that I was ready for our relationship to take that next step, even to the point that I recall a time that she came to the condo with everything she possessed, and I had to send her back home. Well, eventually I gave in. We had talked about getting married but hadn't done so yet. She and my boys were getting to know each other more all the time and seemed to be growing in their relationships.

One difference that came to my attention immediately was the fact that I kept everything very simple in the condo, nothing hanging on the walls, basic furnishings, and just enough kitchen utensils to get by.

Well, Marilyn approached all of that with a very different concept when she eventually moved in. Almost immediately, she was hanging pictures and redecorating our home.

CHAPTER 13

Becoming one in Christ

> So then, they are no longer two but one flesh. Therefore, what God has joined together, let no man separate.
>
> —Matthew 19:6

SHORTLY AFTER I was saved, I was somewhat surprised to become a part of the church leadership participating in meetings, teaching, and other things that were expected of me. It wasn't long after Marilyn moved in with me that Pastor Hale asked me to meet with him.

He came right out and asked if Marilyn and I planned on getting married. I told him, probably so in the near future. He said, "Do you know you are living in sin?"

Oh my, that hit me like a boulder. I said, "You know what, we are, aren't we?" I went home that day and shared with Marilyn what our pastor had said and told her we needed to get married.

We moved very quickly by asking Pastor Hale if he would marry us, and he responded by saying he couldn't as the Assembly of God would not allow divorced people to be married by their pastors. So we asked around about alternatives and were told about a Presbyterian Church and pastor out by one of the bayous that might be willing to marry us. The bayous in Tarpon Springs are known for the Easter ceremonies in the Greek church that take place, where several young men dive into the waters to retrieve a cross after it has been thrown therein. Hundreds of people come annually to watch these services.

John and Marilyn's Wedding photo L-R Lex T. Robertson, Sr. and wife Joyce, Marilyn, John, Johns Mother, Irene and Jim Barnette

We set up a meeting with the pastor of this church, and he agreed to officiate at our wedding. We set the date for October 30, 1982. We asked Pastor Paul and his wife, Elizabeth Hale, if they could participate and sing at our wedding, and they said they could, and we were thrilled to hear them say that. The song they sang was "There Is Love."

The church was full of family and fellow workers and people from church. One couple from church was Lex and Joyce Robertson. God works in wondrous ways. Shortly after joining the church, I found out that they had a softball team. I thought, *Wow, that's cool. I think I will join them.* Lex Robertson was the coach. And as we were walking from the parking lot to the field for our first practice and talking, I asked him where he was from.

To my amazement, he said Edgerton, Ohio, which was just a few miles from where I grew up in Edon, both being in Williams County.

Our softball team was very good, and we won two championships while I was a member and playing catcher and shortstop at various times. My son, Toby, was an outfielder, and we loved being on the same team.

This all just increased the bond that Lex and I had as fellow brothers in Christ even more. Well, Marilyn's parents could not be there for the wedding, so she asked Lex to walk her down the aisle.

As I stood there, watching this beautiful young lady coming toward me, I knew that I had made the right decision and that the past was the past, and it was time to move forward with our lives. I was in love once again!

House in Tarpin Springs, FL where John and Marilyn lived when they got married in 1982

We decided to move out of the condo into a nice home in the suburbs that we found for rent. During this time, we got into a pretty regular routine of church, family, and work. Then after a short while, we purchased a beautiful small stilt house at Crystal Beach. At about this same time, my fifteen-year-old son, Tim, had moved in with us, and his brothers Troy (sixteen) and Tyler (thirteen) visited on a regular basis.

My oldest son, Toby (eighteen), had gone on to college after graduating with honors from Tarpon High School and worked part-time on the Pinellas County sheriff's department as a corrections officer. Crystal Beach was right on the Gulf of Mexico, and our home was about one block from the beach, which was very nice.

John and some Bufkor associates boarding a
private plane for a trip to El Salvador

We were still attending the Assembly of God Church in Tarpon Springs and had developed a very close relationship with the body of Christ there and especially with our pastor, Paul, and his wife, Elizabeth Hale. So we asked for prayer and direction, not knowing what to expect but trusting in God.

Marilyn had several times said she would like to have a child of our own. By this time, I was forty-one years old, the father of four, and just didn't feel that I wanted to start another family. But I finally gave in to the idea. Well, at the same time, we found out that Marilyn was pregnant, but a few weeks later, she had a miscarriage.

John with a Bufkor Associate at the Bufkor South facility in El Salvador

We decided that she probably couldn't get pregnant and carry to conception. In her conversations with Sister Hale, the discussion turned to adoption as she and Brother Hale had adopted their two boys, and her mother held an executive position at an adoption agency for unwed mothers that was founded through the Assembly of God Church in Florida.

We discussed and prayed more about it and finally decided to apply. After about three months, we received word that we had been accepted to be the parents of an unborn child, whose mother had given it up for adoption upon birth.

She was very early in her pregnancy, so we knew we probably had a fifty-fifty chance that this young girl could change her mind at any time up until the papers, giving up her rights to the child, were signed after the birth in about six months.

Bufkor South American Manufacturing Plant

Around this time, I also got to go to Guatemala and Honduras, South America, to visit SigmaQ's manufacturing plants. This is the company that had just purchased Bufkor.

I had recently met a banker by the name of Eric Welman that I became very close to, and we were meeting on a regular basis for breakfast or lunch. At one of these meetings, he asked me if I had ever thought about going into business for myself. I told him that was always in the back of my mind.

He then proceeded to tell me that he had recently been introduced to Steve Carlton, the Hall of Fame pitcher known as Lefty, who had just left the St. Louis Cardinals and joined the Philadelphia Phillies, who had spring training in Pinellas Park. Steve had just signed the first million-dollar contract ever in baseball history and was looking for ways to invest his money.

I told Eric that I would consider starting up a jewelry display manufacturing company because of the experience I had developed over the past couple of years in manufacturing and in communicating and getting to know many different customers, both large and small. He said, "Let's both think about that and get back together in a week."

When the week had passed, we met, and Eric said that Steve would like to meet with me. During that meeting, I found out that he had a building in Port Richey, Florida, that had been made available to him. He asked if I would like to go and see it.

We scheduled a time to do so, and to my surprise, when I was introduced to the owner, it was Pistol Pete Maravich, the Hall of Fame basketball player. What an experience for this little old country boy to meet two famous people so quickly in this new walk. Everything looked like it would work fine for what we were thinking about, so the next step was for me to lay out a business plan.

It took me a couple of weeks because one thing I wanted to be sure of was that we had some business in place. I talked to my contacts at Sears and Kmart about them being providers and gave them both a quote on various items that they would need. Once the quotes were accepted, we would be ready to proceed. After only a few days, I got a positive response from both, and we made the decision to proceed with the formation of the new business.

I submitted my resignation to Bufkor and then took the next steps in this journey. Now we had to get some folks hired and all the equipment in place, along with the inventory we needed. I talked to my good friends, Jack and Sandy Stiverson, about joining us, and initially they said yes but shortly afterward decided not to.

I then thought about Lex Robertson from church, who had been the GM at Edgerton Forge in Edgerton, Ohio. We met, and

Lex said yes! Marilyn had enough experience in the covering area of the product in manufacturing to put her in charge of that, and we proceeded building our business.

My position was VP/CEO and minority stockholder of Creations Unlimited of Port Richey, Florida, a jewelry display manufacturing company. Everything was going well. We were growing and adding new clients on a regular basis with around twenty-five total employees.

It was at this time that, as I was returning from a business trip to New York, Marilyn called me during one of the layovers to tell me that our son, Joshua Eugene, had been born in Plant City, Florida. We were scheduled to go pick him up a few days later at an attorney's office there. What an exciting time for both Marilyn and me in our lives together. A few weeks later, we had Josh dedicated to God at the Tarpon Springs Assembly of God Church.

I had always heard that you love an adopted child as much as a naturally born one, and I can tell you, this was very true from the moment we laid our eyes on him. The next step that God had planned for us was to find out that Marilyn was three months pregnant with our youngest son, Caleb.

Then one day, a board meeting was called, and I was informed that Steve, the majority stockholder, had decided to sell the company to one of our strongest competitors. During this transaction, I was told that they would be bringing in all their own management team, which meant of course that Marilyn and I were gone.

CHAPTER 14

Where Now, Lord?

Praise be to the God and Father of our Lord Jesus Christ, the Father of compassion and the God of all comfort, who comforts us in all our troubles, so that we can comfort those in any trouble with the comfort we ourselves have received from God.

—2 Corinthians 1:3–4

GOD CAN TAKE our adversity—a heart attack, cancer, an automobile accident, violent crime, bankruptcy, a marriage crisis, the loss of a loved one—and transform that pain into encouragement for the people around us.

We come out of those experiences stronger and better able to comfort others. What great lesson to learn in our lives. I now had to stand on God's word and direction.

While we were starting Creations Unlimited, we also purchased a beautiful small stilt house at Crystal Beach. A stilt house is one that is built in an elevated fashion to protect it from floods and storms. We could drive our car right up underneath it to park. Crystal Beach was right on the Gulf of Mexico, and our home was about one block from the beach, which was very nice.

Not knowing what to expect but trusting in God, of all the career options that I was seeking, the one that materialized for the time being was car salesman. Ugh! I hesitantly proceeded in that direction with a local new car dealership and went into training on how to sell cars. Everything went well, and I found myself consistently being in the top group of salesmen.

We started to have conversations about moving back up North, which was a major decision. My older boys were now all teenagers and doing very well, so leaving them was difficult but not as challenging as if they were younger. Marilyn's mom and dad said we could move in with them until we found a house of our own, so that certainly was a big help.

Finally, the decision was made, and we prepared to move. Here we were with a small baby and Marilyn eight months pregnant, and we were on the way to making another major change in our lives together. We started packing and rented a U-Haul, which our son, Troy, just seventeen years old now, would drive for us. From Tarpon Springs, Florida, to Columbus, Indiana, was a fourteen-and-a-half-hour trip that totaled approximately 955 miles, quite a trip for Marilyn watching over Joshua and being that far advanced in her pregnancy with Caleb.

I had been in Florida for four years and liked it but was ready to return up North, even though Columbus would be much different than Edon.

Two things from that trip back up North stand out in my mind. The first is that the U-Haul that Troy was driving broke down in Tennessee, and he had to call the company for a replacement and then transfer everything from one vehicle to the other. Quite a responsibility for a seventeen-year-old, but he told us to keep on heading North, and he would be all right.

As it worked out, some strangers stopped to help with the transfer of our belongings, and he was soon able to continue his way.

The second thing was that as Marilyn, baby Josh, and I were crossing the bridge over the Ohio River at Louisville, Kentucky, we had a flat tire. It was three lanes wide, and I had no choice but to stop in the middle lane. Here I was with my family, stuck in rush hour with a decision to be made, but I really had no choice but to unload everything that we had packed into the trunk and change the tire. I said a quick prayer and quickly got to work. As I got out of the car, I realized that I had stopped on the grated area, where you could look down and see the water and the boats below.

I was amazed at how high up we were as I am not a fan of heights. To my amazement, some other cars stopped behind us, and several men started to direct traffic and assist in any way that they could. God answered my prayers once again. To my amazement, through this whole process, no police or emergency personnel or vehicles of either kind were involved, and I know that traffic was backed up quite a distance behind us.

God was in control. And as we proceeded for the next couple of hours, we finally reached our destination. Troy arrived safely the following day, which was another answer to prayer.

CHAPTER 15

Back to Where Marilyn Grew Up and Then on to Where I Grew Up

> The Lord directs the steps of the Godly. He
> delights in every detail of their lives.
>
> —Psalm 37:23

IT WAS THE fall of 1985 when we arrived at the Hitch's for a new chapter in our lives. Patsy, Marilyn's sister, said she had a good friend, Steve Fletcher, that owned a dealership in Edinburgh, which was just a few miles north of Columbus, and that if I needed a job, I should go see him. A few days later, I did so and started my career at Fletcher Chrysler and Jeep immediately. That was a big hurdle as I was wondering what I would be doing. And with a baby boy and another child on the way, I wanted to be sure we had a steady income.

Because we had been attending church on a regular basis, one of the first things we did was locate the Assembly of God Church in Columbus. We attended there for a little while, and after a few weeks, we heard about a house in a subdivision a few miles away from Marilyn's parents that was available, so we went to see it and made an offer on it right away.

It was a nice one-story home with a full basement, and we loved it. After a while, we started attending the Assembly of God in Seymour, Indiana, just south of where we were living. The one in Columbus was just too big, and we didn't feel the connection there that we were searching for. Caleb was dedicated to God in this church!

Once again, we fell into a regular routine of church, work, and family, spending a considerable amount of time with Marilyn's parents and siblings. I enjoyed working at Fletcher's and meeting different folks daily. One thing about Southern Indiana, it seemed more country than anywhere else I had been—by that, I mean people just acted very down to earth most of the time.

November finally arrived as we were anticipating the arrival of our youngest son, Caleb. Then one day at work, I got a call from Marilyn that she had started labor, and her mother was taking her to the Columbus hospital.

It was a very long process, but when she delivered him twenty-one hours later, it was well worth it. I was in the delivery room, which was a first for me as when the older boys were born. They did not allow the dads to be that close to the process.

A few days later, they came home, and Josh, even at seven months old, seemed excited. The thought of these two being so close in age made me think it would almost be like raising twins. A few weeks later, we had Caleb dedicated at the church in Seymour just as we had Josh dedicated in the church in Tarpon Springs.

About three months later, at a routine wellness check, we found out that Caleb had a heart condition, patent ductus arteriosus, a heart defect caused by problems in the heart's development that would require surgery. But they could not do the surgery until Caleb reached the age of twelve months (one year).

His condition was such that an extra artery that all babies have while in the womb, and by three months of age, that extra artery closes off, as it is no longer needed. In Caleb's case, that artery did not close, which meant that his blood was not pumping through his heart properly and needed to be surgically closed. At that same time, we had started talking about moving to Edon, which was a major decision for Marilyn.

In May, we did make the move to a beautiful old house in town, known as the Maxwell house, which was owned by the son of a lawyer in Bryan, Ohio, that I had known. I had been offered a job in Fort Wayne, Indiana, working in sales from an industrial supply company and started it the same week that we moved. Everything seemed to be going fine for us.

We found a church in Montpelier, Ohio, by the name of Soul's Harbor, pastored by Jan Garber and his wife, Marlene. It was a great spirit-filled church, and we enjoyed attending there. One memory was that Marilyn had a miscarriage during a Sunday morning worship there. She was heartbroken but came through it all stronger than ever.

At that church, a couple of weeks later, when the offering plate was being passed around, the Holy Spirit told me to reach into my billfold and put what was in it into the offering plate. All I had in it was a $100 bill. My first reaction was, *What?* But the Holy Spirit spoke again and said, "Do it," so I did trust in the Lord

I had maintained a great relationship with Leon Segal the VP of sales at Bufkor, and we communicated on a regular basis. We were talking on the telephone one day, and he said that our biggest competitor had just been sold out, and the new owners were seeking some staff. He said, if I was interested, I should call Don Parks, the founder of Chippenhook.

CHAPTER 16

On to an Opportunity of a Lifetime

Stop being deceived; God is not to be ridiculed.
A person harvests whatever he plants.

—Galatians 6:7

SO THE VERY next day, I prayed for God's will and then made the call to Don Parks. Our conversation went very well, and he invited me to fly down to Dallas, Texas, for an interview. He said they would schedule the flight and pay all expenses, including a hotel during my stay. We proceeded accordingly, and then the day came for my departure and visit.

I had to drive to Toledo Airport for my flight. I had never been to Dallas, Texas, so I was excited to see it. From Toledo, I flew to O'Hare Airport in Chicago, Illinois, where I had to change flights. O'Hare Airport was amazing in size, but I just followed directions and got to the proper gate for departure to Dallas.

I enjoyed the flight there and was thinking of how things had progressed since I accepted Jesus as my Lord and Savior. The progression that God had brought me through to get to where I was heading to Dallas and everything regarding my career during this time just seemed to be all a preparation for what He had in store.

When I got to Dallas, I was picked up by Dennis Crawford, who was executive vice president of design and marketing and had previously been employed by Bufkor prior to joining Chippenhook. He took me to a hotel just outside of Flower Mound, Texas, which is a suburb of Dallas, where Chippenhook's corporate offices were located.

Dennis returned the next morning to take me to the Chippenhook headquarters and manufacturing facility, where I met Don Parks face-to-face for the first time. He introduced me to the CEO, Larry Johnson. Don took me on a tour of the facilities after a short conversation and introduced me to several key employees. I was very impressed with everything I saw and everyone I met.

Then we went back to his office, and he told me what they were looking for was someone to take over the Midwest territory in sales as regional sales manager and asked if I would be interested. The territory would consist of Ohio, Indiana, Michigan, Illinois, and Kentucky.

The pay was very good, and I would receive a monthly expense check. Remember my statement earlier about the $100 in the offering and trusting in the Lord? God is true to His word!

He invited me and several of the key people to his home that evening for dinner and told me that I could give him my final decision then. It turned out that his home was several miles out into a rural area. One thing I remember is on the way there, we had to stop as a herd of longhorn cattle were crossing the road.

Upon arrival, I found the home to be a very elaborate and beautiful structure with an outdoor pool and gazebo. Everyone was gathered on the patio between the house and the pool, chatting and having a great time, along with enjoying the great food that was served.

When Don walked up to me, he introduced me to Barry Rutherford, president and CEO, and Jack Towle, VP of sales, and then asked what I thought and if I had made a decision. I responded with, "I am very impressed, and my decision is yes."

One thing that was shared with me by the national sales manager, Jack Towle, in a very kind and professional manner, was what they expected of their company representatives in appearance. We were expected to be clean shaven, with fresh haircuts, and to dress like the men models in the then-famous GQ magazine. I thought right away, *Well, there goes my Fu Manchu mustache and my long hair.* I also knew that I would have to go shopping and update my wardrobe when I got back home.

That night back in my room, I was thinking about the direction my life had taken and what an awesome God we serve. I'd never functioned in the world with the type of people that I was dealing with now. When I called Marilyn and shared with her, she was excited as well. We would now be able to improve our livelihood in a big way.

I spent one more day at the facility, talking about the samples that I would need for sales presentations and everything else related to this new job before boarding a flight back home.

Once home, I got a haircut and shaved, then went shopping. I set up a small office and took a few days to evaluate everything to come up with a game plan to cover this vast territory. I had responsibility and access to every client, large and small. We had a large directory, showing everyone that sold jewelry that was provided by the jewelry industry, so I started to review each of my states.

Sidenote: I recently had the opportunity to talk with Andy Macauly, who was the advertising director of Chippenhook, and he brought back so many wonderful memories and gave me the names and numbers of a couple of people that worked in customer service that he said would like to talk with me. Remember this was around twenty-four years after I left this fantastic company. The respect and kindness that we shared with one another will forever be with me.

Within days, I realized that I was receiving credit from corporate for every sale that was made in my territory. Up to this point, the company had been doing approximately $150,000 annually in these five states. Along with my salary and expenses, I was to receive 10 percent of all sales, which was a very generous compensation package in my mind.

I was very eager to get started in this new career. The sales experience that I had acquired over the past years would prove to be very beneficial as I proceeded forward. The company sent new leads to me daily and copies of orders that were received for my follow-up. I initially focused on Ohio as that is where we lived, and I wanted to get a feel for everything before going out further in my territory.

I prayed daily for direction and guidance, both in my professional life and in my personal walk with Him. At this same time, a house a couple of blocks from where we were renting came up for sale at a very reasonable price. It was an older Victorian-style home that needed a lot of work, but we saw a lot of potential in it and proceeded to purchase it.

Shortly after, we moved in. It was time for Caleb to go to Toledo for his heart surgery. It was 1986, and he was a year old now. Thank God, everything went well, and he mended quickly.

CHAPTER 17

An Amazing Experience Careerwise, But...

Do not be conformed to this world, but be transformed by the renewal of your mind, that by testing you may discern what is the will of God, what is good and acceptable and perfect.

—Romans 12:2

WE PROCEEDED TO remodel this old Victorian home and bring it back to life. It was right behind the Lutheran church that I grew up in and across from the park under the old water tower. We could walk to any business in the downtown area with ease! The house turned out great.

Right next to it was a preschool, where Josh and Caleb both attended while we lived at this location. We had recently bought them a couple of those little battery-powered vehicles that they could drive, and a few times, at the age of approximately four and five, they drove them to preschool.

I scheduled trips each week to cover my territory, normally being on the road from Monday through Thursday, calling on accounts. Things were going well as I called on independent jewelers then started stepping up to call on major accounts, like Sears, Montgomery Ward, Dayton-Hudson, and many others.

One day, I set an appointment and stopped in at the corporate offices of Sterling Inc., which consisted of Kay and Zales Jewelers, which had always done business with our competitor, Bufkor. As I entered the lobby and walked up to the receptionist, I was somewhat overwhelmed with what I was doing, so I said a prayer and moved forward.

The gentleman that I was to meet with came out and got me and took me to his office to discuss their jewelry display needs. The amount that they used to install in new stores or to replace worn items was astonishing to me. Finally, he gave me a list of items to quote on, and I then thanked him for the opportunity and left.

When I got to my car and was opening the trunk, another gentleman came running up quick and introduced himself as Robert Knapp and asked if I had any box samples with me. I answered, "Absolutely," and he asked me if he could see them right there in the parking lot without even going to his office.

After viewing them, he showed me which ones they use and what fabric and color they were done in and asked if I could get him a quote ASAP. They had over a thousand stores at that time and the quote for approximately five hundred thousand boxes. I was flabbergasted, to say the least. As I left, I thanked him and then headed toward home on the turnpike as it was now Thursday. I decided I should call corporate and share the news of this great opportunity and did so. They couldn't believe their ears. Everything fell into place perfectly, and they became our biggest client.

I was asked by corporate to go to Mexico and spend a few weeks to help set up a manufacturing facility there.

I remember that we crossed the border through Brownsville, Texas, and drove several miles into Mexico to get to our destination. It was a great experience, and I truly enjoyed it. One memory was the first day I was there. And when it came time for my lunch, the GM told me where I could go to get a bite and said they specialize in chicken and beef.

When I returned, he asked me what I ordered, and I told him beef. He and everyone around him started laughing, and he said, "You just ate dog meat." I guess the joke was on me!

As my income increased substantially, we started of course spending more money on material things and decided once again to move. We found a nice ranch-type home north of town, about five miles that set back in woods. After going to see it, we decided that we would like to move there. After negotiating a price, we made an offer and put the Victorian house up for sale.

We now had approximately five acres and a lot of privacy to raise our boys on. The house had three bedrooms, two baths, and a fireplace in which I loved burning fires and sitting beside.

I planted twelve blue spruce along the edge of the backyard, and we built a small barn. Twenty acres that were attached to the south became available, and we purchased that, bringing our total acreage to twenty-five. What a beautiful place God had provided us with. But as I look back, I question if we really appreciated it. The job had provided us with much.

As things developed in this new career, I found myself traveling even more. I was visiting corporate in Dallas at least six times a year, along with doing industrial shows in New York City; Las Vegas, Nevada; and San Diego, California, at least twice per year. Then I was asked to speak at jewelers seminars in major cities around the country.

One trip to New York stands out as while I was flying first class and had boarded the plane, I turned to my right and couldn't believe who was setting behind me and across the aisle. I got excited and asked the stewardess if that was really Coretta Scott King, Martin Luther's widow. She responded by saying, "Yes, it is. Would you like to meet her?"

I said, "Oh no, don't bother her."

A few minutes passed by, and the next thing I knew, Coretta was standing up beside me and asked if she could sit down to chat for a minute.

I was in awe and said, "Sure you can."

We had a great cordial discussion, and she invited me to the Martin Luther King memorial in Atlanta and gave me a number to call before I came down so she could take me on a personal tour.

I then pulled a small Bible out of my briefcase and asked her if she would autograph it, which she did. When I got home, I donated that Bible to the Edon library, and regretfully, I never did make it to the monument, which I have always regretted.

Many of my travels were scheduled over the weekends, so I started to miss church on a regular basis. Whenever I could, on all my trips, I would search for a local Assembly of God Church and attend, if possible, but that seemed to be getting more far apart.

Without me being there every Sunday, it was also a challenge for Marilyn with the two young sons to attend on a regular basis. I would take Marilyn and the boys with me on these business trips periodically.

CHAPTER 18

Focusing on the Things of This World and Losing Sight of God

Examine yourselves as to whether you are in the faith. Test yourselves. Do you not know yourselves, that Jesus Christ is in you?

—2 Corinthians 13:5

Exchange students Francisco (Pancho) Hidrobo (Ecuador) and Sondra Milena Herrera Ramirez (Columbia)

ON THE HOME front, we had seen ads about exchange students and thought that would be kind of cool, so we checked into it. We decided to apply and were approved for an exchange student from Ecuador to come to the USA for his senior year of high school.

His flight arrangements were made, and we were scheduled to pick him up at the Fort Wayne Airport on August 30, 1990. Josh was five, and Caleb was four.

When Francisco "Poncho" Hidrobo got off the plane, we recognized him immediately. When we went up to welcome him, we were amazed with the fact that he knew very little English.

We took him home and managed with our communication just fine, got him enrolled for school that fall, and moved forward. Poncho learned our language very quickly and later told us that Josh and Caleb helped him with that as much as anyone. I remember the first time it snowed after he arrived; how excited he was to see snow for the first time in his life. He went out and stood in it with his arms outstretched for the longest time.

He was very popular in school and was a great soccer player. We didn't have soccer at Edon, so we made arrangements for him to play at Hamilton, Indiana. He stayed the full year and became family to us, and we, to this day, call him our son, and he calls us Mom and Dad.

On June 7, 1991, I drove him to the Toledo Airport in my new Red Corvette, so he could depart to Houston, Texas, to live with his brother. Over the next few years, he maintained his legal status as a citizen of the United States of America. It is awesome how he has progressed with the Caterpillar Corporation to become one of their top executives.

As things continued to flourish, we started buying new cars on a regular basis, along with different toys for the boys, bikes, etc. The money that was now coming in had us focusing on these material things a large percentage of the time, and our focus on God was gradually dwindling.

We still attended church on a regular basis but certainly not like we had in the past.

We also had one more exchange student, who came to live with us in the fall of 1991 for six months. This time, it was a young lady from Columbia, South America. Her name was Sondra. She was a very quiet young lady, and we enjoyed the time that she was with us too.

On my business trips to and with corporate, we ate out a lot at the finest restaurants in the country. With our meals, many times wine was ordered. Then afterward, everyone would sit around and socialize with a drink or two. It wasn't long until I found myself participating in these activities too. And along the way, a client offered me an expensive cigar to smoke as we walked around the terrace of the hotel, and I lit it up and smoked it. This was all in the beginning of my backsliding into the things of the world.

My territory was doing fantastic as I brought aboard many major accounts, like Sterling Jewelers, Jared, Kay, Zales, Sears, JCPenney, Montgomery Ward, Dayton-Hudson, and many more, along with increasing our independent jewelers accounts. When I first started, as I stated earlier, the territory had done $150,000 maximum. A few short years, I had taken it to $3,500,000 and been named salesman of the year several times. I had established a reputation in the industry that was admired by many and envied by some.

House on 40 acres in Fremont, IN

Winright house and 40 acres in Fremont, IN

Everything was going so well that we decided to move up once again. We sold our place and bought a forty-acre farm with a brand-new 3,500-square foot, two-story home. It sat back a lane and was located on the Ohio/Indiana state line a quarter of a mile south of where Michigan joins the two states.

It had five acres of woods and a stream running through it, with a wooden bridge crossing to the back four acres. A few months later, we had a seven-acre pond put in and stocked with fish.

6-acre lake that John built on his 40 acres in Fremont, IN

Josh and Caleb had ATVs, dirt bikes, a paddle boat, and all kinds of other toys. I bought Marilyn a new red Buick convertible with a white top and bought myself a new four-door green Mercedes. How could we do all this? I was making in the high $100,000 to low $200,000 per year in the 1990s. That was a lot of money back then.

We had about everything that anyone could dream of and were living a life in the world instead of in Christ. I was traveling constantly during the year but normally had extra time off between November and January each year.

Many times, I would take Marilyn and the boys with me. I had a big part in working with my clients at the Mall of America in Minneapolis, Minnesota, when it was being built. At that time, it was going to be the largest mall in the world. One time, when they were getting close to completion, my family came along, and we stayed at a beautiful ski resort.

When the mall was finished in August of 1992, it had 330 stores and ten thousand employees. We went up when it opened so I could do follow-up calls with my clients, and while there, we enjoyed the amusement park that was built inside, especially the roller coaster.

Winright-Strobel reunion—meeting new family members for the first time

Back at the farm, we had a family reunion every year with a picnic, fishing, camping, hiking, and playing golf on a one-hole temporary course that I had made out in front of the house. We even gave a trophy to whoever teed off and was closest to the hole.

I not only mowed the yard around the house but had a bigger tractor to mow the whole farm and did so on a regular basis. I loved to mow and enjoyed doing it tremendously.

We also had a nice garden plot that we planted each year. Many mornings, we would look out the back windows and see herds of deer grazing and playing among themselves. It was a beautiful place and atmosphere to live in.

William Carlyle Winright, John's oldest brother

Even though we were now living in Indiana, it was right on the state line, so we worked it out with my former basketball coach, who was now superintendent of the Edon School District for Josh and Caleb to continue school there. Kent also arranged for the bus to pick them up. That meant a lot to the boys and to Marilyn and me as they would not have that part of their lives disrupted.

On Thanksgiving, in the year 1997, we were invited to my sister-in-law Patsy's house, and I thought it would be a great opportunity to go on down to Charlotte to participate in the NASCAR Racing Experience, which we planned to do after we left Patsy's.

But while we were there, I received a call, letting me know that my brother, Bill, had passed away at the age of fifty-seven. This of course was a big surprise and heartbreaking, so we made plans to return home. His funeral was in Montpelier, Ohio, and he was buried in the family plot at the cemetery there. It was very hard losing my first sibling.

CHAPTER 19

Getting Our Priorities Back on Track with Our Lives

Search me, O God, and know my heart; Try me, and know my anxieties; And see if there is any wicked way in me and lead me in the way everlasting.

—Psalm 139:23–24

AS WONDERFUL AS everything was going, the Holy Spirit started working on me in a big way. Every time I turned around, it seemed like I was being convicted of something. My family was doing great as my older boys were moving along with their lives.

Toby had gotten his bachelor's degree at South Florida and his master's at Duke. He was now attending Notre Dame, working on his doctorate. Tim was into the cabinet manufacturing and installing business and had become known as one of the best in the tristate area. Troy, after being in the navy, ended up managing airports and became VP of operations in Titusville, Florida, close to where all the astronauts take off for flight into space. Tyler kind of followed in his father's footsteps in manufacturing, ending up in high management positions with a few different companies. As their father, I of course was very proud of them all.

It seemed like each day that passed, the Holy Spirit kept talking to me, and I kept resisting to listen to what He was saying. I loved my job and everything about it. Chippenhook was without a doubt the best company that I had ever worked for and the most rewarding one.

The thing the Holy Spirit kept asking me was, "Is it really worth it?" I really didn't want to have this conversation, but after a short time, I started to think about all the worldly things we had gained compared to all the spiritual things that we had put aside—not attending church on a regular basis, backsliding into things we should not be doing, not praying or reading my Bible on a regular basis. Was I putting myself and my family into a precarious position as far as where we would be spending eternity?

The Bible is clear when it comes to where we spend eternity and *how* we get there.

> Whoever believes in the Son has eternal life; whoever does not obey the Son shall not see life, but the wrath of God remains on him. (John 3:36)

> For the wages of sin is death, but the free gift of God is eternal life in Christ Jesus our Lord. (Romans 6:23)

These verses started penetrating my spirit daily. I knew that I had a decision to make. What would Marilyn and the boys and the rest of my family and friends think? And what would Chippenhook's reaction be? I finally took a major step and got down on my knees and prayed about it.

Nothing changed right away as I continued to do my daily scheduled activities and travel, remaining the top regional manager in total sales. I was still amazed that God could bring me so far from that small-town farm-boy atmosphere. One thing that has always amazed me is how I got more opportunities once I moved away from home to further my career than I ever had at home, maybe just because there were more of them.

Winright Enterprises - Custom Cabinets and Jewelry Display Recovery

In the fall of 1997, I was scheduled to go to the annual industrial show for our products in Las Vegas, Nevada. I was to fly out that Friday, and I was really being influenced by the Holy Spirit to resign and get back to being the Christian that I was called to be. I knew that if I proceeded according to the Holy Spirit, we would have to downsize tremendously in everything.

Winright Enterprises employees recovering jewelry displays

Another factor was that we had just recently purchased a building in Edon to start Winright's Custom Cabinets for my son Tim to run. This was a major investment in equipment and everything, but we had a pretty good customer base and actually built some jewelry showcases for a couple of my clients. The decision boiled down to, do I want what I think is good for me, or do I want what God has planned for me?

Jewelry displays recovered at Winright Enterprises

I really wasn't on a time line or anything but was feeling compelled to decide. I finally gave in and called Doug Campbell, the VP of corporate sales, and told him I would not be going to Las Vegas as I was resigning my position. He said, "What? Are you crazy? You are our top guy!"

I said, "It is just something that I need to do!"

CHAPTER 20

Be Obedient in All Things

> But happy is the man who has the God of Jacob as his helper, whose hope is in the Lord his God.
>
> —Psalm 146:5

I ALMOST WISH that Thomas Jefferson had not written about the pursuit of happiness. He was right that we should have a right to pursue happiness, but the problem today is that people are pursuing happiness without knowing exactly what they are looking for or where to find it.

True happiness begins when one is in a relationship with God. He is the true source of happiness in contentment, security, peace, and hope for the future. None of these can be found in a job, a human relationship, money, power, or position. They are God's alone to give. That is why Jesus, in His Sermon on the Mount, told where the ultimate happiness lies when He said, "Happy '*are they who hunger and thirst after righteousness, for they shall be filled.*'"

I wanted back that true happiness that I had when I first accepted Jesus Christ as my Lord and Savior in Tarpon Springs, Florida, on that cool crisp February evening. From a worldly standpoint, that meant that my family and I would have to sacrifice the things that we had turned to for happiness and start seeking the things of God and His will. We needed to step out in faith, trusting Him.

Then he went and joined himself to a citizen of that country, and he sent him into his fields to feed swine.

And he would gladly have filled his stomach with the pods that the swine ate, and no one gave him anything.

But when he came to himself, he said, "How many of my father's hired servants have bread enough and to spare, and I perish with hunger!

I will arise and go to my father, and will say to him, 'Father, I have sinned against heaven and before you, and I am no longer worthy to be called your son. Make me like one of your hired servants.'"

And he arose and came to his father. But when he was still a great way off, his father saw him and had compassion, and ran and fell on his neck and kissed him.

And the son said to him, "Father, I have sinned against heaven and in your sight, and am no longer worthy to be called your son."

But the father said to his servants, "Bring out the best robe and put it on him, and put a ring on his hand and sandals on his feet.

And bring the fatted calf here and kill it, and let us eat and be merry; for this my son was dead and is alive again; he was lost and is found." And they began to be merry. (Luke 15:15–24)

I can truly relate to the scriptures above because God, my Father, did the same for me and delivered me out of a backslidden condition.

I found a job in Coldwater, Michigan, as sales manager for a company that sold parts for customizing and lifting pickup trucks. The pay was much less than I had been receiving, so we started making plans on cutting back and positioning ourselves to proceed in a much different fashion than we had been living. This meant selling our beautiful home and farm, getting rid of all the toys, and buying a much cheaper home to live in. Over the next few months, we liquidated everything and moved to Edon, Ohio, once again.

When we got settled in, we began to search for a church to get back into the realm that God wanted for us. We eventually ended up at the Butler Assembly of God, which was located between Edgerton, Ohio, and Butler, Indiana, on Route 6.

I had to release everything to God, step out in faith, and believe that He had a plan for us! I just needed to trust in Him. Only believe, and never give up. I was already starting to feel good about getting back to where we should be as children of God and away from the material things of this world.

Another aspect of all of this was family. I probably actually ignored the family that God had blessed us with over the past few years. My wife, children, and grandchildren are very important to me.

We did move once again to a home on the other side of town, known as the Frank Walz house, which was formerly owned by a prominent citizen by the name of Frank Walz, who had six daughters, two of which were in my class in school. Leanne and Deanne were their names. The home was one story, with a huge living room, three bedrooms, and two baths.

Caleb Winright with his Rookie of the Year Modified race car

It was now 1998, and we just needed to stay in His will daily and see what He had in store for us. Josh, Caleb, and I had, for the past few years, attended races at Angola Motor Speedway and Butler Motor Speedway up by Quincy, Michigan, carrying on the family tradition that I had mentioned earlier in this book. We had many friends that went too, and some of them were drivers that we knew. Caleb mentioned that he would like to drive a race car once or twice, and the next thing we knew, we had a Street Stock sitting in our garage.

Caleb's 00 Modified race car

The next thing we knew, we were participating in the races each week. In 1999, Caleb won Rookie of the Year in the modified division. He absolutely loved it, and I believe he inherited that from my dad.

We were becoming very involved in our new church home, and I was asked to be a member of the board, and Marilyn was asked to take over the girl's Missionette program. We loved attending this small church out in the country. Matthew Snodderly became pastor there shortly after we joined and was an on-fire spirit-filled preacher, who truly preached the word of God each week.

In the year of 2000, having lived back in my hometown for a while, the pending election was coming up, and I decided through much prayer to enter my name for the position of mayor. Edon was a small village of approximately one thousand folks.

John Lee Winright being sworn in as Mayor of Edon, OH in 1999

On the night of the election, Marilyn and I went to the county seat in Bryan to await the results. To my amazement, I won by 374 votes. The election was in September, and I would be sworn in and take over my new duties in the following January. Governing a small town along with the council members was a lot of responsibility and a great learning experience and another step toward the goal that God had planned for my life.

CHAPTER 21

Another Venture into the Unknown by Being Obedient to Him

> Trust in the LORD with all thine heart; and lean not unto thine own understanding.
>
> —Proverbs 3:5

DURING MY TENURE as mayor, we completed the installation of a new water tower one mile north of town and consistently came in under budget each year, thanks to the cooperation and help from everyone on the council and in the village. Another great memory from that time was I got to be involved in putting up a sign at each end of town on the highways and at the entrance to town, honoring Dave Herman, whom I had mentioned earlier, a member of the New York Jets Super Bowl team.

I had continued in my friendships at Chippenhook and, in 2003, got a call, asking if I would be interested in taking over the Southeastern United States and the Islands off the Florida coast. Arrangements were made to go back down to Dallas to corporate to discuss in greater detail with Barry Rutherford, the president. After much discussion, I agreed to do so.

I went back home and discussed it with Marilyn and the boys. Josh was entering his senior year of high school and did not want to leave. As difficult as it was, we planned for him to move in with our son Tyler and his family so that he could have his wish. This was one of the most heart-wrenching decisions that we made. Then I turned in my resignation as mayor with one year remaining on my term, and we listed our house for sale.

Another challenge was leaving the Butler Assembly of God Church, as we had grown so much in the time we attended there. But as I had learned up to this point, pray and trust the Lord in all things.

A coincidence in all of this was that Caleb had continued to race and was recently given an opportunity in South Carolina to drive seven truck races for Don Hawk, who had been president of Dale Earnhardt Sr.'s racing program. This was an opportunity that few people get, so it seemed to fall in with the overall move that was being presented.

After doing some research, we decided to move to Gaffney, South Carolina, which lies right up by the North Carolina line, about 65 miles southwest of Charlotte, North Carolina, and about 45 miles south of the Blue Ridge Parkway. We found a real old-style country home to rent and moved into it upon arrival. It was a unique piece of property, and I really felt like a Southerner for the first time in my life. Folks in this area seemed so loving and caring for one another.

Over the years we lived there, we loved going to Lake Lure and Chimney Rock, just across the state line in North Carolina, and to go up and drive across the Blue Ridge Parkway and stop periodically to see the streams and waterfalls.

At Lake Lure, we loved eating at the restaurants beside the stream that flowed beside it, watching the water cascading over the rocks and boulders. God's beauty of His creation was everywhere. We would go to the Chimney Rock site and climb up to the top of the four-hundred-foot waterfalls and look down over God's creation in awe of what He had done.

I set things in place for covering this new territory as Marilyn set up the home, while Caleb followed up on planning to meet with Don Park and get things moving on his scheduled truck races.

When we first arrived and were driving around the community of Gaffney, we came upon a university in town by the name of

Limestone, and on campus was a chapel that was having temporary services for the local Church of God while they were having a new facility being built on the outskirts of town. We felt very strongly that we should go there the next Sunday to check this church out. They were a part of the Church of God out of Cleveland, Tennessee, so I knew that their beliefs paralleled strongly with the Assembly of God church.

When Sunday came, we headed to the campus to go to church at the chapel. When we entered, we were greeted warmly and met Pastor Jim McClure and his wife, Angie. We knew right away that we had found a new church home.

As we settled into our new routine, I traveled my new territory, and Marilyn and Caleb set up the house. Caleb met with Don Park and got seven races scheduled in the truck series at Hickory Motor Speedway, which is very historical and where all the old-time NASCAR drivers seemed to get their start: Myrtle Beach Speedway, Charlotte Motor Speedway (dirt track) and Cherokee Speedway, our local track in Gaffney. Everything went well, and we really enjoyed this experience over the next year.

When it was all said and done, it came time for major sponsorships, which was a tremendous challenge. Through a friendship that Caleb developed with a regional late model champion, Dennis "Rambo" Franklin, he got a ride in a super late model and raced against many of the upcoming NASCAR, such as Jeremy Clements, the Dillon brothers, Bubba Wallace, and others. This created some great memories and carried our family tradition in racing even further.

One of the things I really enjoyed in covering my new territory was traveling to the islands as I had never done so before. They were beautiful. And each time I went there, it was on a cruise ship, which was a new experience and very enjoyable.

A year went by, and Chippenhook was sold to their competitor Bufkor, which had their own sales force, so once again I found myself out of work. After praying about it, I went back into the car business with a local dealership by the name of Burns Chevrolet. This turned out to be a comfortable situation and provided us well enough to get by.

Marilyn went to work at Hamrick's, a local department store with locations throughout the Southeast. Caleb did not feel comfortable with attending the huge high school in Gaffney after coming from Edon, so he studied at home and went and got his GED, then he also went to work at Hamrick's on a part-time basis and soon bought his first car, a 2001 Mustang.

Josh seemed to be doing okay back home, but we missed him tremendously. Our church, Covenant Christian Center, finally moved out of the chapel and into our new church building on the edge of Interstate 84 in Gaffney. It was a beautiful facility, and we were very excited about it. Marilyn and I had become involved in many things in the church once again and loved every moment of it. Caleb was a part of the youth program and established some lifelong friends.

I became a part of the church staff and got to teach and preach periodically, and Marilyn became involved in the Missionette program. We also sang in the choir in every service. The talent in music in this church was amazing. We loved this church, and once again, the people in the South are amazingly friendly.

Over the course of the next few years, we moved a couple of more times, eventually ending up at a home about six miles out of town on about ten acres with seven of it being woods, with a stream running through it. It was a beautiful piece of property with three bedrooms, fireplace, and all. I had recently gone to work for Dick Brooks Honda as their Internet sales manager.

Dick Brooks was a famous NASCAR driver. His son-in-law was the president of the dealership and a great person to work for. The dealership sold around two hundred cars a month and was very well-known throughout the area. I had never worked in the Internet side of the business, so it was a learning experience. As things turned out, I became very adept at it, eventually setting records several times monthly.

Caleb had gone to work up by Charlotte Motor Speedway for a company by the name of Carbotech which manufactured brakes for the racing industry all around the country. He eventually became a supervisor. They also participated in racing shifter carts at the Charlotte road racing course, and he and his team won a couple of championships.

Future home of William's Garden, a camp for
autistic children in Gaffney, SC

About this same time, Pastor McClure turned in his resignation at the church and was replaced by another pastor. This was devastating to me as Pastor Jim and I had become very close friends. For some reason, my spirit just did not relate to the new pastor, so I decided to attend another local church, which was much larger.

Gaffney couple filling a need
William's Garden will serve children with autism

By JOE L. HUGHES II
Ledger Staff Writer
joe@gaffneyledger.com

Wanting to shed light on an ailment becoming more prevalent among youths both locally and abroad, a Gaffney couple has committed to do all they can to help these children live long, productive lives.

Already having raised their family and nearing retirement age, John and Marilyn Winright have formed William's Garden, a nonprofit organization whose purpose is to serve youths between the ages of 5 and 18 in Cherokee County and surrounding areas who are diagnosed with autism.

"We kind of saw a need in the community for some kind of program to help our children," Marilyn Winright said. "Looking at special needs, particularly autism, the need is there and there is a difference we can make."

Autism is a developmental disorder that appears in the first three years of life, affecting the brain's normal development of social and communication skills. Typically, parents realize something is wrong with autistic children by the 18-month mark. Most make the determination and seek help by the child's second birthday.

Symptoms consistent with the ailment often include sensitivity to sight, hearing, touch, smell and/or taste, unusual distress when routines are changed, tendency to perform repetitive body movements, and showing an unusual attachment to certain objects. The symptoms can range from mild to severe.

Autism affects boys three to four times more often than girls.

With few avenues present locally to help aid children dealing with autism and their families, Marilyn Winright believes William's Garden can fill a void.

"Families whose children are autistic are forced to travel to Spartanburg, Columbia or Charleston to address their needs," Marilyn Winright said. "That's particularly why we are beginning something here so we can do things to provide resources for children and their families."

Among those resources is 16-acres of land to be turned into a summer camp for autistic children, offering opportunities for hiking, fishing and swimming activities, as well as horseback riding and other activities. The local couple hopes to have the camp up and running by next year.

Using much of their funds to create the help group, the Winrights are hoping to receive a little help from the community in achieving the goal.

"The cost of filing for exempt status has proved to be much more than expected... we personally paid all expenses up to this point but need help now to raise funds for the filing fee," Marilyn Winright said.

For more information, call the Winrights at (864) 812-7153, (864) 812-7557, or visit www.williamsgarden2010.com.

Williams Garden Ledger Article 09-27-10

New Harvest Fellowship, with Pastor Robert Wells and his wife, Rhonda, is where we went and almost immediately knew that is where we belonged. It was about three times larger than our old church but still had the feeling of love and compassion shared by everyone there. Everything about this spirit-filled church was dynamic, and a great move of God was experienced continually in the services.

We had been thinking for some time about starting a camp for autistic children on our property, and as we were, a tragic event appeared in the local newspaper about a young boy walking away from his home and disappearing to later be found drowned in a local river.

His name was William, so we decided to name our camp William's Garden. We proceeded to get many kinds of animals for the camp, as that was one thing the children loved. We had horses, chickens, rabbits, a potbellied pig, and many other animals.

Feb 22, 2011 John and Marilyn accepting a
$1,000 donation for William's Garden

When Christmas came, we had a Christmas dinner for the parents and kids. This was one of the most memorable experiences of the whole project. Marilyn and Caleb were teasing me that when it came time for me to speak that they didn't think I could do so without getting choked up. I responded by saying "Sure I can." Guess what, I got choked up. Seeing the joy on each child's face as they went up to the tree to get their presents and the tears in their parents' eyes was just too much for me. I did struggle, but thankfully, God made it through okay.

Campsite at Williams Garden, Gaffney, SC in the Fall

We were now entering our tenth year in South Carolina, and Marilyn one day said that she wanted to move back north to be close to family, which had grown substantially over the years. She told me she would like for that to happen within a year. My response was, "If that's the case, why wait?"

CHAPTER 22

God's Ways Are Greater Than Ours

"For My thoughts are not your thoughts, Nor are your ways My ways," says the LORD.

—Isaiah 55:8

John's 6 sons L-R Caleb Carlyle, Tyler Clinton, Tobias Lee, Troy Thomas, Joshua Eugene and Tmothy John Winright

OUR FAMILY NOW consisted of Toby and Liz and their two girls, Claire and Lydia; Tim and his son, Wyatt; Troy and his daughter, Abbey; Tyler and Cindy and their daughters Morganne, Mercedes, and Maime. Toby and his family lived in St. Louis, Missouri. But the rest of our children lived in the immediate area.

I went online to search for a home we could buy and found one out west of Fremont, Indiana. I talked to the owners, and we negotiated a ten-year land contract at a very reasonable price. Once again, it was a major move in our lives but, as always, stepping out in faith, trusting God, not knowing what He had planned for our lives. "Trust in the Lord with all of your heart, mind, and soul."

> In all your ways acknowledge Him, And He shall direct your paths. (Proverbs 3:6)

We rented a U-Haul, which I drove, while Marilyn and Caleb both drove our cars. Caleb had gotten into breeding and selling pit bulls while living in South Carolina, which had been very profitable for him, so we still had a couple of them that moved with us. Upon arrival, we got settled in, and I went to work at Haylett RV in Coldwater, Michigan.

We now started to search for another church to call home. There are many fine churches in this tristate area to attend. We went to Jamestown, Fremont community, Angola Assembly of God, Soul's Harbor, Coldwater Assembly of God, and several others, looking for a home church, at the same time, working and establishing our lives back in this area. It was kind of neat after being gone for ten years to be experiencing what we were with family and friends.

We also got to see my sisters, Bonnie and Judy, on a regular basis and attend all the family holiday activities that they had. And my mother had moved in with them, so we got to see her too. They all lived in Montpelier in a nice home on the northside of town. We also had our first great-grandson, Chance Helmuth, which was great, and Marilyn even got to babysit him on a regular basis.

During this time, the Holy Spirit spoke to me and reminded me of how many times in my life that He had called me into the ministry. It seemed like every ten years, something came up, reminding me of when I was attending catechism at the Saint Peter Lutheran Church as a thirteen- or fourteen-year-old and Pastor Donald Good looking at all the boys there and saying, "Someday, two or three of you are going to be pastors."

Of course, at that time, we all kind of laughed and teased one another about what he had said. Over a course of time, Robert Young and I did enter the ministry.

"God can qualify the unqualified" is something that I had read and given a lot of thought to. He reminded me of all the different directions He had taken me in my life and told me that everything I had been through was in preparation for what He had planned for me all along. About this time, I decided to start taking online classes in theology from Dallas Theological Institute.

I also applied for ordination from the National Association of Christian Ministers and, after going through the proper procedures, received my ordination papers.

It was great to be back home after ten years and to be able to see family on a regular basis once again. I had just received my ordination papers, and within a few weeks of returning, my granddaughter, Morganne, asked me to marry her and Catlyn Helmuth in a country setting out north of Angola.

It was a beautiful wedding, and I was honored to be able to perform the matrimony. My mother, Irene, who was now getting up there in years, was also present. It was a very big wedding, and the setting in a barn atmosphere was beautiful.

We were getting settled in and establishing a regular routine. Caleb was working for a local manufacturing concern, and everything was going well. Josh had gone to and graduated from Defiance College and was working his way up the ladder at the company he worked for in Toledo, Ohio.

I had started attending a Saturday night get-together called the Gathering at a local gym downtown for Christian folks from various churches in the area. We took turns speaking each week, and this truly was a blessing at the time. There also was a gathering place in Fremont called the Firehouse for the youth in our and surrounding neighborhoods and communities. That was very dynamic.

Through this, we met a couple by the name of Joel and Peggy Wernert, who had a ministry in downtown Angola by the name of Solomon's Porch, and we were blessed to know them.

The day came that I told Marilyn that since we had not found a church that we could call home, the Holy Spirit told me that we were to start a church.

When your memories are bigger than your dreams, you are headed in the wrong direction.

> In the last days, God says, I will pour out my
> spirit on all people: your sons and your daughters
> will prophesy, your young men will see visions,
> your old men will dream dreams. (Acts 2:17)

The enemy always attacks in situations like this, and believe me, he did. He had me questioning if I could really start and pastor a church, especially with the history that I had lived in my past life. But God reminded me that I am a new creation in Him.

So I started to look for empty churches around the area to see if we could start a church in one of them. I looked at one in Ray, Indiana, and talked to the owners, but nothing worked out. I went to Silver Lake, west of Angola, and looked at one, but that fell through.

I ventured up to Kinderhook, Michigan, to look at a church there, only to find out that it had just been sold and was going to be turned into a home. I guess Satan was afraid of seeing anything happen. But the more I looked, the more convinced I was that this was God's will.

CHAPTER 23

Once Again, Only Believe and Never Give Up

> The fear of man brings a snare: but whoever puts his trust in the Lord shall be safe.
>
> —Proverbs 29:25

In Solomon's Porch (The Porch) in Angola IN where Revelation Chapel Began June 30, 2013

I STAYED IN prayer daily and was being told by the Holy Spirit to relax and be patient and to trust in the Lord. So I went about my daily business and work, trusting in Him. I needed to be patient and know that if God has a plan, it will happen on His time line and not mine. For some reason, the only thing I visualized was a church building and nothing else.

Then one evening, when Marilyn and I were at the storefront downtown Angola that housed the Solomon's Porch, Joel and Peggy Werner were sitting at a table with us, discussing our situation, when all at once Joel smiled and slid a key across to us and said, "Start your church here." *What? In a storefront and not a church building? Okay, Lord, if that is your plan, we will be obedient.*

We went home and started to discuss what we were going to name the church and a couple of days later came up with Revelation Chapel. This was late in the year of 2013, and we were extremely excited to see what God had planned for His church.

Our first service was on Sunday, June 30, 2013. So at the age of sixty-nine, I finally answered my calling as founder and senior pastor at this church, stepping out in faith, believing that God would bless His church if we confirmed continuously that it was His church and that He would be in control. This would be a book of Acts church that would be Pentecostal and spirit-filled in every way. An Acts 2 upper room church with no doctrines and not under man's influence in any way—I was honored and humbled just to be a small part of it.

Our first service drew about twenty folks, who were a combination of family and friends. Everything went very well, and we were blessed. From that day forward, we had services every Sunday morning.

Rell Myers, whom I had mentioned earlier in a previous chapter, called me one day, expressing his excitement after hearing about our church. Before hanging up, he said that maybe some Sunday he would come and visit us. A few weeks later, as was my normal custom, I was out walking around the block, praying over our upcoming service, when a car pulled up beside and stopped and rolled their window down. To my amazement, it was Rell and a friend of his.

He asked me where he should park, and I told him to go around back, and I would meet him there and show him. As he got out of the car, and we greeted each other, he then reached inside his jacket and pulled out a piece of paper and said, do you remember this? To my amazement, it was the letter of apology that I had sent to him after I was saved.

When we went inside for the service, I introduced him to everyone, and then he read that letter. It brought everyone to tears, including me. What an awesome God we serve, and what a great impact this man of God had on me.

> Blessed are those whose way is blameless, who
> walk in the law of the Lord! (Psalm 119:1)

To me, this was Rell.

We continued to have services at this location with about ten to twelve people attending on a regular basis as we saw salvations, healings, and miracles happen on a regular basis. God was blessing us continually. During different community events that happened in the downtown area, we received some attention and made our presence known. Sometimes our worship team would sing during these events, and people would stand by outside or come in to listen to the great gospel music.

After being at this location for several months, we were made aware of a place in the basement of the Odd Fellows Lodge that might be available to us.

I set up a meeting to see the facility and to discuss in greater detail with the top people in this lodge, and we came to an agreement on rent and everything involved and made the move to this new location.

The Odd Fellows building in Angola IN where
Revelation Chapel moved to in 2014

The building had a rear parking lot and entrance that was very sufficient for our needs. Inside, we had a full kitchen and two bathrooms, along with a large area for fellowship and meals and another area for our services. It was much larger than the downtown location, and we felt that God was opening another door for the plan that He had for His church.

Revelation Chapel in the basement of The
Odd Fellows building 10-15-2014

When starting a church, you must know that it is God's will and that you may experience many challenges along the way. You must "trust and obey," as the old hymn states—faith, faith, faith, and more faith! Each step must be looked at as a step forward and not backward.

It was at about this same time that I left Haylett RV and went to work in maintenance at the outlet malls, north of Angola and east of Fremont. This involved maintaining the premises inside and out and was something that I ended up enjoying.

We also had a chance to sell our home and to buy one in Angola on Powers Street, down close to Trine University. Moving back to town was somewhat of a challenge, but everything worked out fine.

My son, Tim, had recently given me a bike, and I started to ride it on a regular basis on a route that I established that ran from our house out past the high school and back, and I learned to really enjoy doing this and piling up several miles of exercise monthly.

Shortly after moving, I had the opportunity to go to work at Bon Appétit in the cafeteria at Trine University as a supervisor. This also was a great experience being around all the students, professors, and leaders on campus.

We fell into a pattern of regular services at the church, along with helping to present and promote different ministries that came to be a part of our church and to share their ministries at the same location. One was Fire and Glory, with Virgil and Wanda Long on Thursday, Friday, and Saturday nights for several months. These were powerful, spirit-filled meetings that touched many lives.

Another was Step by Step Ministries with Jim and Carla Barbarossa, which was a great ministry of sharing testimonies. We would meet once a month, and a few people would be chosen to stand up and give their testimony in a five-minute presentation.

A big part of this ministry was the writing and publishing of personal testimonies in several different editions of *Lighthouse* real life stories that would be handed out free to hundreds of thousands of people around the world. It was my honor and privilege to be asked to share my testimony in the third edition of these publications. I believe they are now up to around the fourteenth edition.

The church would sometimes vary somewhat in attendance. One Sunday that I will always remember is when Marilyn and I got there and prepared everything for the service. We noticed that no one had arrived yet. We had been running up around fifteen people. We waited and waited, and finally a car pulled into the parking lot.

One lady walked into the church, and we waited until our starting time and decided to go ahead and proceed with just Marilyn, her, and me in attendance. Stepping out in faith, knowing that God was in control, we did everything as we normally would: opening prayer, offering, praise and worship, sermon, altar call, and dismissal.

In all honesty, I could not look at this in the natural and had to believe that through the supernatural power of God and by being obedient to Him, everything would be all right. The following week, our attendance was back to normal, and we proceeded from there in faith.

On June 23, 2015, we got a call that Marilyn answered, and it was the rest home that my mother was in, letting us know that she had passed away. My mother had led a very good life raising us kids and surviving heartbreak. She was very strong-minded and a loving, caring person. She lived ninety-five years and was a blessing to us all.

CHAPTER 24

Another Step in God's Direction and Plan

> "Declaring the end from the beginning, and from ancient times things that are not yet done, Saying, 'My counsel shall stand, And I will do all My pleasure,' Calling a bird of prey from the east, The man who executes My counsel, from a far country. Indeed, I have spoken it; I will also bring it to pass. I have purposed it; I will also do it."
>
> —Isaiah 46:10–11

ONE AFTERNOON, WHILE reading the local help wanted adds, I saw an ad for a position to manage the day-to-day operations of the Welcome Center in the southbound lanes of Interstate 69 at mile marker 344, working for Arc of LaGrange, Indiana.

This welcome center is about halfway between the Angola and Ashley exits. After praying about it and asking for God's will to be done, I applied for the position and got hired.

During this time, my son, Troy, started having many issues and experienced a heart attack. He lived in Florida and managed the airport there that I mentioned earlier, so we made a couple of trips down to visit him during his recovery. Then his health was taking a turn for the worse as he was diagnosed with cancer. He retired from his position and moved to Angola for a while then made another major move to Arizona. We went out to visit him a few times in Arizona.

In 2018, we received word that the Odd Fellows Lodge was for sale. The price tag was out of our reach, but we were told we could stay until it was sold. Thus, I felt that we had to start looking once again for a location to move to, remembering that God was in control.

One building that came up was an abandoned church on Mill Street. I decided to meet with the realtor there and to look the place over. I found it to be very interesting and saw some potential in it. I asked a couple of other people to come and look at it at a rescheduled time. We did so and were praying continuously for God's plan and will in all this. There were some concerns with cost, repairs, and parking.

Then one night, the Holy Spirit told me to go back up and talk to the people at the church in Ray, Indiana again.

I called and set an appointment with the pastor and met with him at his home which was on the lot behind the church. The church was an older historical church, having been built in 1876, and the sanctuary still stood. Along with that, in recent years, a very nice fellowship hall had been added on the west side and a classroom section, with four nice size added to the east side.

At the front of the sanctuary were stained-glass panels that had been imported from Germany and then donated by a local banker several years previously. The church had been vacated for about seven years but was in surprisingly good shape.

The pastor and I talked about a price and whether it could be purchased on a land contract. He said he would get with his board of directors to discuss and get back with me.

A couple of days later, he called me and said the board agreed to a three-year land contract with a sale price of $70,000. The contract stated $550 per month, with balance to be paid in full at the end. Also, the $500 per month would be deducted from the selling price upon exercising the purchase.

I told him that I would like to invite people from the congregation to come up to look the property over, and we would pray about it and get back with him. This church sits on the Indiana/Michigan border, out in the middle of nowhere, surrounded by a large Amish population.

After being in a nicely populated area, this was a big decision to make. I had to feel totally comfortable that it was God's plan for His church, Revelation Chapel.

After praying and trusting God, we stepped out in faith and moved forward with the purchase. What an exciting time for all of us at Revelation Chapel to be making this move. Upon receiving the keys, we immediately went to work preparing for our first service.

The pastor and board had expressed to us that the well might need primed or even possibly need a new pump motor as they had been having some issues with it. We started working on it, priming and so on, and were not gaining any ground. After much prayer, we decided to call a couple of well drilling companies to see about getting it repaired as we were planning on having our opening service within the next couple of weeks.

Once again, I had to trust God that everything would be okay. I got online to find a well drilling company in each bordering state of Indiana, which of course included Michigan and Ohio. Upon finding the numbers, I called three well drillers, one in each state. The first one that came was from Michigan. He looked everything over and said, "John, that old two-inch well needs to be replaced with a new five-inch well."

My first thought was, *Oh no*, as I had done some research and knew that the cost for this would be anywhere from $18,000 to $20,000, depending on the depth. I thanked him and told him that I was going to call a couple of more companies to see what they could do as we just did not have that kind of money at our disposal.

The second company I called was from Ohio, and when he got there, he gave the same scenario as the gentleman from Michigan.

As he was leaving, he asked me who else I had contacted. I told him the Michigan one had already been there but that I had not contacted the Indiana one yet. Upon sharing who the one in Indiana was, he immediately said, "Do not contact him under any circumstance. You will be sorry if you do."

I shared everything with the men in the church who had been working on the well, and they went back at it again without coming up with any positive results. I was thinking, *Oh my, we made this purchase and decision, wanting to have our first service in a week. What now, Lord?*

Revelation Chapel of Steuben Co. IN

A couple of nights later, I woke up in the middle of the night, and the Holy Spirit spoke to me, telling me to call the third company in Indiana. The next day, I prayed more about it and then made the call. We set a time to meet for when I got home from my secular job.

Upon arriving at the church and introducing ourselves to one another, we proceeded to walk around and go over everything. That's when this gentleman told me the same thing as the other two. I told him that we just didn't have the funds to move forward. His response was, "How do you know? We haven't even talked price yet."

I told him that through research, I knew what the approximate cost would be.

He then asked me a strange question: "Could you afford a $65 fee to get a permit from the county for a well?"

I said, "Sure, we can afford that."

He told me to proceed with that and then give him a call.

Original stained-glass panels at Revelation Chapel Steuben Co. IN

When I got home, I shared with Marilyn what had taken place and told her, "I don't know why, but I have a feeling this gentleman is up to something on giving us a very special price" and then asked her if she would go get the permit and post it at the church while I was at work the next day.

That afternoon, I gave this gentleman a call and told him we had the permit and asked him what he had in mind on the cost of going from a two-inch well to the new five-inch well. The first thing he said was, "We will furnish all the labor at no cost to you."

I said, "Wow, that is answer to prayer."

Then he said, "We will furnish all of the material at no cost to you."

I said, "Are you serious?"

He said, "Yes, and we will also provide the well pump in the well and the pressure pump inside the church at no cost!"

I was flabbergasted, to say the least, and the lump in my throat made it difficult to speak. He then proceeded to tell me that he would have a crew on site the next day so that we could have our first service the following week, as scheduled.

When a person needs confirmation that they are in God's will, it can come in many ways, but this confirmation that this was and is

God's church was one of the most powerful confirmations that I have ever seen. I knew that we were a part of a great move by God.

In my conversation with this gentleman the day they started the well, I found out that he was a huge baseball fan and had his office walls covered with professional players and their autographs.

I then asked if he ever heard of Steve Carlton, and he said, "John, he was my favorite all-time player and the only one who's autograph I never had."

I then shared with him about having been in business with Steve for a short period of time when I lived in Florida. He was really impressed that I had that privilege. I then asked him how much longer he would be there, and he said probably for another hour or so. I told him that I had to run home for a minute but would like for him to wait for me until I returned.

When Steve Carlton and I were in business together, he was still playing baseball with the Philadelphia Phillies, of whom he went to when he left the St. Louis Cardinals. The Phillies won the world series while he was there. Steve had given me a baseball for myself and for each one of my sons that had five Hall of Fame players from the Phillies with autographs on them.

I had one in my office up on a shelf at home and felt led to go home and get it and give it to this gentleman.

When I got back to the church, his crew were just finishing up, and he was sitting on the front steps of the church, waiting for me.

I got out of my car and held the ball behind my back as I walked up to him. Once there, I reached out and handed the ball to him. When he saw the autographs, he was absolutely astounded that I would give it to him. I thought, *Are you kidding, after what you did for this church?*

One thing he insisted on throughout this whole scenario was that I keep his name anonymous. What a wonderful gentleman and man of God.

The following week Revelation Chapel, a full-gospel Pentecostal church, had their first service in Ray, Indiana. I knew that everything about this church was in God's will and that He had great plans for this church.

CHAPTER 25

Be Obedient in Everything Pertaining to God

Let the peace of Christ rule in your hearts, since as members of one body you were called to peace. And be thankful. Let the message of Christ dwell among you richly as you teach and admonish one another with all wisdom through psalms, hymns, and songs from the Spirit, singing to God with gratitude in your hearts. And whatever you do, whether in word or deed, do it all in the name of the Lord Jesus, giving thanks to God the Father through him.

—Colossians 3:15–17

Winright Homestead and forever home May 20, 2024

ONCE AGAIN, WE felt led to move, this time to be closer to the church. We put our home in Angola on the market and started to search. The house in Angola sold rather quickly, and in the meantime, we found a small five-acre farm north of Montgomery, Michigan on Long Lake Road that we made an offer on. The offer was accepted, and we proceeded with our move. This is going to be our destination as far as we are concerned. During our time together, Marilyn and I have moved multiple times. This place is truly a blessing to us as we enjoy raising our own beef, vegetables, etc. and being able to live in a truly beautiful setting in Amish country that God has provided us with. As I look back over these years, I now see them as the preparation God was making for our lives and service to Him.

The church started off with fifteen or twenty people and Sunday morning services only. One day, a few men who had attended the church a few years back came to meet with me, and we instantly bonded. They shared that they would be coming to visit for a service soon, which they did, and have become a very important part of what God is doing at Revelation Chapel and have invited many folks to come to our services. It wasn't long until we added Sunday night services and Wednesday night Bible study to our agenda.

On October 20, 2017, I had the honor of marrying our son, Josh, and his fiancée, Jessica Glover, at a beautiful outside setting at Tamaron Country Club in Toledo, Ohio.

Troy had now left Arizona and moved back to Florida, where, on February 7, 2020, he passed away at the age of fifty-one. On my last trip down to see him a couple of weeks prior to his passing, he reassured me that he had accepted Jesus Christ as his personal Lord and Savior. As difficult as this was, losing one of my sons, I did have a peace in my spirit, knowing that he was now in heaven.

John preaching at Revelation Chapel of Steuben Co. IN

Revelation Chapel is a very special and unique church. The Holy Spirit showed me early on that the church was surrounded by guardian angels and covered with His blood. He also told me that it would be a church of love and encouragement, and it certainly is.

We begin our services by telling everyone to welcome one another with a smile, handshake, or hug, and sometimes this can take up to fifteen minutes. But that is okay as we are being obedient to Him.

Our services are led by the Holy Spirit, so we are not always locked into a routine, and our preaching is led by the Holy Spirit in every way. When we have a closing prayer, we form a big circle around the sanctuary and join hands.

We have seen many miracles over the years that we have been having church in this great church that is God's, both for individuals and for us as a church. The well story that I told earlier was absolutely a miracle from God, and now I am going to share another mighty miracle that happened for the church. This miracle is another confirmation from God that He is in control. And if we follow and are obedient to Him, anything is possible.

We had been in Ray, Indiana, for three years when our option to purchase was due. We had paid $10,000 down on the church during this time and saved another $30,000 to go toward the purchase, so I felt we were in great shape for a loan at the local bank. With our $30,000 and the loan of $30,000, we would have it covered. I set an appointment and did all of the paperwork to apply for such. A couple of days later, I went in to check to see how things were progressing, when I was told that they could not approve the loan for a small church.

This absolutely caught me off guard as I felt we had plenty of equity toward the purchase. I went into prayer, and the Holy Spirit told me to share with the church body what had happened.

It was stated by one of the members that we should see how much we could come up with from the folks in the church. Another option was to go back to the land contract holders and ask for an extension.

To my and several other's amazement, we had the additional $30,000 within a few weeks and scheduled a time to close on the property. This absolutely was another miracle in God's plan for His church, and we are still rejoicing to this day. Our God is a supernatural God. We must never limit Him with our fleshly thinking.

> And Jesus came and said to them "All Authority
> in heaven and on earth has been given to me."
> (Matthew 28:18)

Many, many times, I wonder how God laid the groundwork for me to found and preach at His church.

"Why me, Lord? What have I ever done?" I am so humbled to be a part of His plan and His church.

Preaching every Sunday for all these years has been such a blessing, and we are the happiest we have ever been in our lives.

Many people will question how and why we would give up the great occupation, income, home, and material things that we did. The answer, as I know firsthand, is, those things do not bring true happiness.

In 2022, our son, Tim, was diagnosed with terminal cancer. This certainly was another heartbreaking experience. Leading up to his death on January 30, 2022, one day after his birthday, we had the opportunity to have several serious conversations, one of which was the true meaning of salvation.

Just a few days before his passing, he told me that he had accepted Jesus as his Savior. Just as it did with Troy, this gave me a peace that passes all understanding. We scheduled a funeral service for him at Revelation Chapel, and I prayed that God would give me the courage and strength to do it, and He did. The church was full of family and friends, along with many from our body of Christ. God heals the brokenhearted.

> And Jesus said unto them, Because of your unbelief: for verily I say unto you, If, ye have faith as a grain of mustard seed, ye shall say unto this mountain, Remove hence to yonder place; and it shall remove; and nothing shall be impossible unto you. (Matthew 17:20)

Nothing is impossible including stage 4 breast cancer.

After going through the suffering, loss, and heartbreak of two of my sons to cancer in 2020 and 2022, right in the middle of this, in 2021, we received more devastating news when Marilyn went for an examination and through it all found out that she had stage 4 breast cancer. This was devastating news to say the least.

Through treatments and much illness over the course of two years and a couple of emergency runs to ER, she survived. The doctors have stated that she is cancer-free. I have never seen someone set a stronger example of faith as she went through hair loss, pain, weakness, and almost death, but she never slowed down from her obligations and responsibilities at the church and for her family and did so with a great attitude throughout.

God still answers prayer, and I am blessed to still have her by my side. I truly don't know what I would do without her.

> The righteous cry out, and the Lord hears them; he delivers them from all their troubles. The Lord is close to the broken-hearted and saves those who are crushed in spirit. (Psalm 34:17–18)

Obedience to God is the key.

Then in August, we got to go to Lake City, Michigan, to perform a wedding for our granddaughter, Maime, and her husband, Bradley Adkins, in another beautiful setting and atmosphere.

CHAPTER 26

God's Ways Are Amazing

Blessed is everyone who fears the Lord, who walks in His ways.

—Psalm 128:1

OVER THE YEARS, God has continually blessed Revelation Chapel in all His ways. We have a church that is debt-free and meeting all the needs that it has daily. We have a body of Christ of true believers that really do show their love for one another. We believe in not keeping what God is doing within the walls of this church but to reach out to all the lost sinners in this world.

> And he said to them, "Go into all the world and proclaim the gospel to the whole creation. Whoever believes and is baptized will be saved, but whoever does not believe will be condemned." (Mark 16:15–16)

The church in Ray has grown to where we will have anywhere from sixty-five to one hundred people attending our services. What a journey of obedience it has been. It has all taken place through the supernatural power and movement of God.

If we would have proceeded in the flesh, God never would have moved in this way. One of the most important things to know is to stay humble and obedient and trust in Him. Never seek the approval of man, and never seek to draw their attention to you. Always point to and acknowledge God in all things.

I also should share at this time how important the pastor's wife is in all of this. A pastor needs the full support of his wife to perform his duties to the fullest. That young innocent girl from Columbus, Indiana, that God sent to be a large part of my life has been amazing in this journey.

Her prayers, support, and hard work have been a true blessing, and without her, this all may not have developed in the manner that it has. I thank God every day for her love and support in my life and that of the churches.

We had over the past few months mentioned the subject of a satellite church and wondering if that might be a direction we should pursue.

We had a ministerial staff in place that could certainly step in if that has ever happened. It wasn't something that took a priority in our thinking but was always there in the back of our minds.

One day, I got a call from a dear friend of mine, who I had known for a long time. Ron Dean and I became very familiar with one another as we went through divorces from our first wives at the same time. We would hang out with each other at the Montpelier Holiday Inn in the lounge and share our heartbreak and many other things with each other.

When I moved to Florida, we kind of lost track with each other but eventually learned that we both had become Christians by accepting Jesus as our Lord and Savior. Our God is an awesome God. One day, Ron called me and asked if we would be interested in obtaining another church. I said we have discussed that in the past, but I just did not know if we were ready to do so at this time.

He told me about a church next to his home that was for sale. It was a church that he had grown up in and was the West Franklin Church of Christ and is in Fulton County, Ohio, about three miles east of West Unity, Ohio, just across the Williams/Fulton County line. After some hesitation, I agreed to meet with him, along with Marilyn, to look.

When we arrived, Ron and the real estate agent that had it listed were both there. The sanctuary was built in 1835, making it a very historical site. In recent years, a beautiful fellowship hall, kitchen, and restrooms were added, and it all sat on approximately three acres. We were very impressed with the facility and all.

Then the conversation turned to the price. The realtor said that they were asking $100,000 for the property, but another church had offered them $80,000, which they accepted. But the church could not attain the financing needed. We knew that the new price was $80,000, but this was still way out of our reach.

As we prayed about it, I told God, if it was His will, please provide the financing needed to do so. In the next week, we asked the pastoral staff if they would go to see the property with us and give us their input. They all agreed to do so and were very impressed with the facility. As we prayed, we basically put it in God's hands and said, "If it's Your will, please provide a way."

It was then that I was told that someone had said they would pay $50,000 toward the purchase, leaving a balance of $30,000 that we would need. That was still more than we felt we could do, so once again, we prayed that if it was His will, He would provide a way.

A few nights later, the Holy Spirit told me to call Ron and ask what he thought about me offering the realtor $50,000, which would mean we would be getting it for nothing but the closing costs. When I called Ron, he said that we wouldn't know unless we tried.

I called the realtor the next day and told him that I had an offer and presented it to him, $50,000. He said he would present it to the seller and get back with me.

He called me the next day and told me they had accepted the offer. What an awesome God we serve that He would provide this fine facility for us at nothing but the closing cost of $250.

I called a meeting of the staff, and everyone was extremely excited but one person. That person brought up many negative thoughts and was concerned about our supporting two churches. After much discussion, I shared my viewpoint on this whole scenario. I told them that I just couldn't see how we could turn down this gift from God.

I felt in my spirit that if we trusted Him, everything would fall into place as He would direct.

Revelation Chapel of Fulton Co. Est. 09-22-2023

The church was down to about five folks attending on a regular basis. And since we were changing from the Church of Christ denomination to a full-gospel church, we would be starting from scratch with attendance. Trust in God in all things. Since He gave us this gift, I just felty that He would bring in the people for this great church, Revelation Chapel of Fulton County.

We went on and proceeded with the closing, and now we are two churches, one body in Christ. It will be exciting to see how God moves in this new location as we proceed down this road. This all took place in September of 2023.

CHAPTER 27

Moving Forward

Put on the whole armor of God, that you may be able to stand against the wiles of the devil. For we do not wrestle against flesh and blood, but against principalities, against powers, against the rulers of the darkness of this age, against spiritual hosts of wickedness in the heavenly places. Therefore take up the whole armor of God, that you may be able to withstand in the evil day, and having done all, to stand.

—Ephesians 6:11–13

John and Marilyn Winright, Founders and Senior Pastor of Revelation Chapel

WE NOW HAD two churches, so we had to plan accordingly. The Holy Spirit spoke to me one morning and said that since I would be turning eighty in the coming month of April, that it was now time to plan for the future of the church.

This meant that we should restructure to be able to function as we should. I prayed about this and was told by my Creator that I should continue as the founder and senior pastor and Marilyn should do so as the pastor's wife and senior administrator and to assign two people to be lead pastors at each location.

This was a major decision for me, and I really had to fight pride and other feelings and concerns to move ahead and share the pulpit and each church with other people moving forward with His plan. He gave me the insight to establish this church with His help and my biggest concern was for other people to understand that vision.

It is His church and not man's. We should never seek the spotlight, and church is not a stage for a show; it is a place of worship. It is all about Him and not man. If we try to draw attention to ourselves, we are not following His will in any way.

I had to trust through prayer and its power that the Lord would place the right people into these two positions of lead pastor.

I followed His plan and picked a couple from our Ray church to pastor the Fulton County church and a couple that attended our church on a regular basis and pastored another church to see if they would be interested in pastoring the Ray church. They both accepted, and we are moving forward for His glory at both campuses.

I am excited to see what God has planned as we move together as one for His glory. We are living in the end-times, so we have our work and assignments to do. Once again, I am so humbled that God would use this little, old country boy with a horrible past as a sinner for His kingdom. I give Him all the glory.

I received this on Facebook messenger from a gentleman that I worked with about forty years ago. He asked, and I confirmed that this was really me. Then he shared this testimony. We never know whom we might impact as a true child of God in our daily walk with Him.

Here's my story: I was doing F and I at Stone Buick, and you were a used car salesperson. One day, I approached you after watching for a while and asked you this question: "What it is that's different about you?" And through that conversation, you invited me to a little Assembly of God Church in Tarpon Springs. I went back to that AOG Church for quite a while, as the pastor was reading my book of life to me every time he spoke. So I always look back at that initial question to you and wish people would ask me that sincere question as well. So here's my thanks to you for being a pivotal player in my Christian infancy.

Since that time, I've been remarried for thirty-seven years. My wife and I have started and supported three pivotal churches in Birmingham, Alabama, the last of which, Church of the Highlands, has over twenty locations and now has an accredited college for growing young Christians into ministries. (K. T. Bowles)

What an amazing testimony, and I find it to be awesome what God has done in this gentleman's life.

Speaking of life, I am now of an age that I look back on mine and would like to share some thoughts about what I have learned on this journey!

CHAPTER 28

With Age Comes Wisdom and Knowledge

> The Spirit of the Lord shall rest upon Him, The Spirit of wisdom and understanding, The Spirit of counsel and might, The Spirit of knowledge and of the fear of the Lord.
>
> —Isaiah 11:2

THERE IS SO much to life and so much to share. We never know how much time we have here on earth, so we need to make the best of every moment. We should not focus on the things of this world, but on God. Sure, we have responsibilities and duties with everything pertaining to our lives, but without Him, we are nothing. We need to be sincere in every aspect of our lives, but *love* is the most important thing.

The Greatest Gift

> Though I speak with the tongues of men and of angels, but have not love, I have become sounding brass or a clanging cymbal. And though I have the gift of prophecy, and understand all mysteries and all knowledge, and though I have all faith,

so that I could remove mountains, but have not love, I am nothing. And though I bestow all my goods to feed the poor, and though I give my body to be burned, but have not love, it profits me nothing.

Love suffers long and is kind; love does not envy; love does not parade itself, is not puffed up; does not behave rudely, does not seek its own, is not provoked, thinks no evil; does not rejoice in iniquity, but rejoices in the truth; bears all things, believes all things, hopes all things, endures all things.

Love never fails. But whether there are prophecies, they will fail; whether there are tongues, they will cease; whether there is knowledge, it will vanish away. For we know in part and we prophesy in part. But when that which is perfect has come, then that which is in part will be done away.

When I was a child, I spoke as a child, I understood as a child, I thought as a child; but when I became a man, I put away childish things. For now we see in a mirror, dimly, but then face to face. Now I know in part, but then I shall know just as I also am known.

And now abide faith, hope, love, these three; but the greatest of these is love. (1 Corinthians 13:1–13)

Without love, we are nothing.

God will allow us to go through circumstances in our lives, which may be difficult, but if we learn from them, it increases our wisdom. As I look back over the years, under this scenario, I should be a very wise person. I welcome the spirit of wisdom and understanding in my life.

CHAPTER 29

We Get One Chance in Our Life Here on Earth—Let's Make the Most of It

Everything Has Its Time

To everything, there is a season,
A time for every purpose under heaven:
A time to be born,
And a time to die;
A time to plant,
And a time to pluck what is planted;
A time to kill,
And a time to heal;
A time to break down,
And a time to build up;
A time to weep,
And a time to laugh;
A time to mourn,
And a time to dance;
A time to cast away stones,
And a time to gather stones;
A time to embrace,

And a time to refrain from embracing;
A time to gain,
And a time to lose;
A time to keep,
And a time to throw away;
A time to tear,
And a time to sew;
A time to keep silence,
And a time to speak;
A time to love,
And a time to hate;
A time of war,
And a time of peace (Ecclesiastes 3:1–8)

WHENEVER I READ these verses, it makes me think about how true these words are and how I personally have experienced all of these in some way.

CHAPTER 30

What I Have Learned

> What then shall we say to these things? If
> God is for us, who can be against us?
>
> —Romans 8:31

ONLY BELIEVE, AND never give up!

Wisdom and knowledge are very important in every area of our lives. You do not need a high IQ for wisdom and knowledge. You need an asset called common sense. As I look over the past eighty years of my life, I realize that I have seen many changes, some good and some not so good.

> Sing, O heavens! Be joyful, O earth! And break
> out in singing, O mountains! For the Lord has
> comforted His people and will have mercy on
> His afflicted. (Isaiah 49:13)

Comfort and prosperity have never enriched the world as adversity has done. Out of pain and problems have come the sweetest songs, the most poignant poems, the most gripping stories. Out of suffering and tears have come the greatest spirits and most blessed lives.

> Behold, happy is the man whom God corrects; Therefore, do not despise the chastening of the Almighty. For He bruises, but He binds up; He wounds, but His hands make whole. (Job 5:17–18)

Setting priorities in our lives is very important. Make sure they are in line with God's word and will for your life, then stand on them and live in them accordingly.

One thing I truly believe is that God is a God of positives, thus I try to be optimistic in everything I do. I have learned that Satan hates this and will try to overpower it with negative thoughts. We need to overcome his attacks and learn to lean on God.

I've learned that the order of things in our life should be (1) God the Father, Son, and Holy Spirit, (2) family, (3) work. In that order, if we follow that pattern, everything will be all right.

Put God first in all things. In my own story, before I accepted Jesus into my life, I was not following that order, and I was a mess. Now, as I look at what He has done because of my obedience, I think, *I really don't deserve what He has done.* I am truly and honestly humbled that He would use me for His glory and kingdom.

Family is so important in our lives. God brought a spouse to share our lives together and children to love and raise as best we can. My family means everything to me. As we progressed through the previous pages and chapters of this book, God blessed me with an amazing family. My wife, Marilyn, and six (6 + 1) amazing sons, along with three fantastic daughters-in-law, and then the children, grandchildren, and great-grandchildren—Toby and his wife Elizabeth (Liz) and daughters Clare and Lydia; Troy and his daughter, Abby; Tim and his son, Wyatt; Tyler and his wife, Cindy (affectionately known as Cinderella), and their daughters, Morganne, her husband, Catlyn, and their sons Chance and Colten, Merceides; and Maymie and her husband, Bradley, and their son, Acre; Joshua and his wife, Jessica (Jess), and their daughter, Riley, and sons Tanner and Brantley; our youngest, Caleb, and Francisco (Pancho) Hidrobo, who came to us as an exchange student in high school but became our seventh son for life and his sons Luca and Nico.

My work history is somewhat mind-boggling, having been involved in so many different careers, varying from janitorial to sales and executive positions. I can see now, as I look back at this, God was laying the groundwork for where I am now. Each experience was a preparation process.

We need to learn how to forgive others. Even our own worst enemies. Once I was saved, I learned this and started praying for forgiveness from everyone that I had done wrong in my life. At first, it was a real challenge. But the more I did it, the better I felt. And if they asked me to forgive them, I certainly did. Through it all, a great burden was lifted form my shoulders.

The joy of the Lord is our strength. The more I pray, read the word of God, and praise and worship Him in song, the stronger my joy grows and the stronger I am!

Give thanks in everything. That means even the hard times you may be going through. We learn from those times, and they make us stronger to face anything that happens in our journey.

Let your light shine in this dark world. Every time I go out in public, I see so many tormented-looking faces. A smile can do wonders for people we come into contact wherever we go. We need to do everything that we can to show everyone we are different, for the Bible says, we may live in this world, but we are not of this world once we are saved because we are a new creation.

Be generous to everyone, and be willing to help whenever you can. We are living in a hurting world, and many people are struggling.

Give 10 percent of your income back to the Lord in tithes and offerings and put another 10 percent of your income back in savings each paycheck.

Whatever you do will come back to you—if good, you will be blessed; if bad, you will pay the price.

Color blindness, when it comes to humans, is very important. God created all mankind, no matter what the color of their skin, and He loves them all equally as we should too. Some of my best friends come from all different nationalities and color.

God can qualify the unqualified and use them for His glory.

I also know that God blessed me with a very loving, caring wife that I love dearly. We have been on a roller-coaster ride for forty-two years, and we have hung on tightly together and learned to enjoy the ride.

In the years that I have left, I want to do everything for His glory and to set an example for everyone who knew me. I love my family, and I love my church family and all my friends. God has blessed me mightily!

The meaning of "only believe and never give up"—read the word of God, believing that it is true, and trust Him in all things. Never give up because He will never leave you or forsake you.

CHAPTER 31

Time Is Running Out

But know this, that in the last days perilous times will come: For men will be lovers of themselves, lovers of money, boasters, proud, blasphemers, disobedient to parents, unthankful, unholy, unloving, unforgiving, slanderers, without self-control, brutal, despisers of good, traitors, headstrong, haughty, lovers of pleasure rather than lovers of God, having a form of godliness but denying its power.

—2 Timothy 3:1–5

IN CLOSING, I just want to share that having lived on this earth for eighty years and seeing what is happening in the United States of America and around the world, almost all the Bible prophesies have been fulfilled, and the rapture gets closer every day. We need to wake up as individuals and realize, now is the time to accept Christ as our personal Savior.

Our greatest achievement in life is to accept Jesus Christ as our Lord and Savior! My ultimate desire is for all my family, friends, and enemies, everyone in the world, to do just that so that they can have eternal life in heaven rather than in hell!

The smartest and most important decision anyone can make is to accept Jesus as their personal Lord and Savior. Bow your head and say the following prayer in all sincerity, and you will be saved!

Dear God in heaven, I come to You in the name of Jesus.

I acknowledge to You that I am a sinner, and I am sorry for my sins and the life that I have lived. I need Your forgiveness.

I believe that Your only begotten Son, Jesus Christ, shed His precious blood on the cross at Calvary and died for my sins, and I am now willing to turn from my sin.

You said in the Bible that if we confess the Lord, our God, and believe in our hearts that God raised Jesus from the dead, we shall be saved.

Right now, I confess Jesus as my Lord. With my heart, I believe that God raised Jesus from the dead. This very moment, I accept Jesus Christ as my own personal Savior. And according to His Word, right now I am saved. Amen.

Only believe, and never give up!
Only believe in the word of God and the Trinity—Father, Son, and Holy Spirit—and you will have the strength to never give up, no matter what you are facing in this life and throughout eternity!
God bless you all!

ABOUT THE AUTHOR

JOHN L. WINRIGHT is founder and senior pastor at Revelation Chapel of Steuben County, Indiana, and Revelation Chapel of Fulton County, Ohio.

John and his wife, Marilyn, have been married for forty-two years and have a blended family of six sons, three beautiful daughters-in-law, ten grandchildren, three great grandsons, and a bonus son, who came to them as an exchange student in high school and became like family to them.

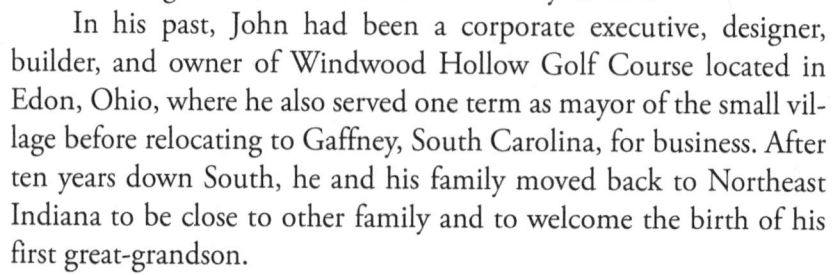

In his past, John had been a corporate executive, designer, builder, and owner of Windwood Hollow Golf Course located in Edon, Ohio, where he also served one term as mayor of the small village before relocating to Gaffney, South Carolina, for business. After ten years down South, he and his family moved back to Northeast Indiana to be close to other family and to welcome the birth of his first great-grandson.

John and Marilyn are now semiretired, remaining very active in both churches, and look forward to spending more time attending sporting events of their grandchildren, gardening, and tending to their five-acre hobby farm in Montgomery, Michigan.

www.ingramcontent.com/pod-product-compliance
Lightning Source LLC
LaVergne TN
LVHW050051070225
802923LV00009B/227